RESPONSE TO INTERVENTION
(RTI)

RESPONSE TO INTERVENTION (*RTI*)

In Indian Context

edited by

Dr. G. Victoria Naomi

To order additional copies of this book, contact:
Xlibris
1-888-795-4274
www.Xlibris.com
Orders@Xlibris.com
757297

Contents

5 RTI in Indian Context: Evidence Based Research 92

Premavathy Vijayan, G.Victoria Naomi,
R.Shanthi, R.Nagomi Ruth and M.Revathi

Foreword

Response to Intervention (RTI) has exploded in the field of elementary education over the past two decades in the United States. For the first time in India, RTI has been implemented in the Public schools in Coimbatore in the State of Tamil Nadu adapting the US model. In the two Indian schools where RTI was piloted, RTI has slowly begun to change the school culture around assessment in a way that no other initiatives were able to do successfully.

Universal screening which is a new concept in India enabled students who need help with learning to read and proficient in mathematics.

RTI emphasizes using assessments to provide instruction in reading and mathematics. This book presents an overview of RTI in Indian context, assessment procedures, preparation of curriculum based measurement, teaching reading and math concepts and the outcomes of the pilot project.

I believe this book can help educators in developing countries to adopt the model and help implement an era of RTI in elementary schools in India and developing countries.

Dr. Premavathy Vijayan
Vice Chancellor
Avinashilingam Institute for Home Science and Higher Education
for Women
Coimbatore
Tamil Nadu-India

Acknowledgement

This Indo-US project consumed enormous amount of work, insight and dedication. First of all we are thankful to the United States India Educational Foundation (USIEF) for the financial support to execute this Research Project. We would like to thank the University Grants Commission, New Delhi for allocating the fund and providing necessary guidance concerning the project implementation.

We are grateful to the authorities of the Avinashilingam Institute for Home Science and Higher Education for Women, Coimbatore, Tamil Nadu which was the Lead institute and the authorities of the Institute of Community Integration, University of Minnesota, USA, the partner institute, for their cooperation, encouragement and provision of infrastructural facilities.

We would like to express our sincere thanks to our research partners Dr.Brian Abery and Dr.Renata Ticha and the US team for their technical support. Without their superior knowledge and experience, the project would not have been completed with the desired outcomes.

We owe our gratitude to the Educational Officers, teachers and students involved in the Project.

We acknowledge with gratitude the contribution made by the authors in the book.

Our sincere thanks to Mrs.Lydia Michael for her Computer assistance.

About the Book

The Book entitled **"Response To Intervention in Indian Context (RTI)"** is the outcome of the research on Response To Intervention (RTI) in Indian Schools.

Chapter 1 gives an overview of RTI, its historical roots and the major components of RTI model.

Chapter 2 portrays the RTI model implemented in Indian Schools. It details the development of measures based on curriculum for assessment of reading and math ability.

Chapter 3 and **4** describe the English Reading and Math instruction in RTI in Indian Context with Illustration.

Chapter 5 highlights the effect of RTI on Reading and Math emerged out of the Indian Research. I am hopeful that this book will serve as a guideline for teachers and researchers to adopt RTI models in schools

- Editor

About the Editor

Dr.G.Victoria Naomi is the Professor, Department of Special Education, Avinashilingam Institute for Home Science and Higher Education for Women, Coimbatore, Tamil Nadu, India. She has been in the field for over three decades having wide and rich experience in teaching children in Inclusive Settings. She has undertaken various researches in the field of Special Education and Inclusive Education. She has authored 10 books and published over 100 articles in the field.

About the Authors

All the Authors of this Book are from Avinashilingam Institute for Home Science and Higher Education for Women

Coimbatore, Tamil Nadu, India.

Prof.Premavathy Vijayan M.Sc., M.Ed.,Dip.Spl.Edn.(U.K),Ph.D
Vice Chancellor

Teacher Educator in Special Education

She was one of the very few pioneers in the country who implemented Inclusive Education in India. She is a Fellow/Member of Common Wealth British Council. She has participated and presented papers at numerous conferences/workshops/seminars. She has authored/co-authored 9 books/monographs and published articles in reputed Journals. She continues to provide reviewer services to a number of journals and edited 3 books in Special Education published by IGNOU (Indira Gandhi National Open University) New Delhi. She has been conducting innovative researches in Education and Special Education for nearly 20 years. She has been honoured with prestigious National award for her **"Outstanding Services for the Empowerment of Persons with Disabilities 2010"** by the President of India Smt.Prathiba Patil on 3.12.2010. She was the Director of the Indo-US Research Project on Response to Intervention Model in Indian Context.

Prof.G.Victoria Naomi M.A., M.Ed., Ph.D
Department of Special Education

She has been in the field for over three decades having wide and rich experience in teaching children with visual impairment in inclusive settings. She has undertaken various researches the field of special education. She has authored nine books and published over 100 articles in the field of Special Educatio. She has undertaken a number of researchers collaborating with International Researches. She was the coordinator of the Indo-US Research Project on Response to Intervention Model in Indian Context.

R.Shanthi MRSc., M.Ed
Assistant Professor (SG),

Department of Special Education,

She has 22 years of service in the field of special education, especially in the area of teaching children's with hearing impairment in special and integrated education. She has published 2 books and 10 articles in International level and 26 in National level and developed the finger spelling for 247 Tamil Alphabet. She was the Project Staff in the Indo-US Research Project on Response to Intervention Model in Indian Context.

R.Nagomi, Ruth M.Sc., M.Ed., M.Phil

Assistant Professor
Department of Special Education
She is possessing Master degree in Mathematics with Master of Special Education. Also having Master of Philosophy in Education with 15 years of teaching experience both in inclusive school and at higher educational institution. She was the Project Staff in the Indo-US Research Project on Response to Intervention Model in Indian Context.

M.Revathi, M.Sc., M.Ed

Special Educator
Research Associate
She is possessing Master Degree in Mathematics with Master in Special Education. She is a Special Educator with 10 years of experience. And also she has rich experience in National and International Researchers. Currently she is working as Research Associate in the Research Project Entitled "Positive Behavioural Intervention and Support for Students at risk for Disabilities in Inclusive School." She was the Research Assistant in the Indo-US Research Project on Response to Intervention Model in Indian Context.

T.Gomathi M.Com., B.Ed

Special Educator
She is a Special Educator in Mental Retardation. She has 3 years experience in assisting special needs students in Computer Application. She acted as Special Educator in the Indo-US Research Project on Response to Intervention Model.

1

Response to Intervention - An Overview

Premavathy Vijayan and G.Victoria Naomi

Response to Intervention (RTI) is a process providing systematic research based instruction and interventions for struggling learners. The instruction or interventions are matched to student's needs and the progress monitoring is continuous. It is designed as an early intervention to prevent long term academic failure.

RTI is based on a three tier model. Tier I is the core instructional programme. In this Tier 80-85% of students cope with the regular curriculum. Tier II - if students do not make adequate progress in Tier I, more intensive services and targeted interventions usually in small group settings are provided in addition to the instruction in the general curriculum (5-10%); and Tier III -for students who do not adequately respond to the targeted interventions in Tier II.

The goal of the instructional modifications is to accelerate the children's rate of growth so that they will be able to meet grade-level expectations. In RTI model, when appropriately intensified and targeted interventions fail to lead to accelerated progress in learning, the child would be considered for possible learning difficulties.

RTI is an evidence-based initiative that seeks to redefine how reading disabilities are identified and addressed within the school system. RTI features a "continuum of increasingly intensive, specialized instruction" that is implemented in the earliest stages of reading development and continued until the end of second or third grade (National Research Center on Learning Disabilities, 2003).

1.1 Historical Roots of RTI

The historical roots of RTI are found in special education research dating back more than three decades: The work of Deno and Bergan in the 1970s is often referenced as the initial pedigree of current RTI elements (National Association of State Directors of Special Education [NASDSE], 2006). Although aspects of RTI appear in many academic areas, most of the research was concentrated in the area of reading. Reading is often a focus of special education research because many students who are at risk for Specific Learning Disabilities experience difficulties in learning how to read. As more and more research on RTI demonstrated that improvements in reading outcomes for struggling students was both practical and possible, momentum and acceptance of this tiered instructional practice and thus resulted in the inclusion of RTI in the reauthorization of Individuals with Disabilities Education Act (IDEA) in 2004 in the United States.

Before 2004, the only recognized method of identifying students with specific learning disabilities (SLDs) was through a discrepancy model in which the main criteria used for determining eligibility was a discrepancy between a student's IQ score and his or her academic achievement levels. This approach was criticized for at least four reasons:

1. A lack of consistency across states in how to measure the discrepancy
2. Ineffective early preventative efforts
3. Absence of instructionally relevant information for educators
4. Possible over identification or misidentification of students with SLDs (Berkeley, Bender, Peaster, & Saunders, 2009)

When the United States reauthorized the Individuals with Disabilities Education Improvement Act (IDEA) of 2004, states were allowed and encouraged to explore RTI as an alternative option to identifying students with SLDs. This approach is gaining widespread acceptance in kindergarten through Grade 12 in many states in the U.S. The RTI model has been piloted in Indian schools with the Indo-US collaborative research project during the years 2013 - 2016. This pilot project was funded by United States India Educational Foundation.

1.2 RTI Definition

RTI has taken many forms. For example, one school's RTI process may include procedures for identifying struggling student through a series of universal screening measures and those students who are at or below the 50th percentile receive an intensive intervention dose for Reading or Math program specifically designed for struggling students. RTI Procedures include assessment, instruction, interventions, and decision making

1.3 Curriculum Based Measurement (CBM)

Curriculum Based Measurement is a standardized process used to assess students' academic progress on a regular and frequent basis which guides in making decisions about students (Deno, 2003). CBM is a broad type of curriculum -based assessment (CBA) and has three Major criteria: (a) materials are associated with the school's curriculum, (b) measurement regularly occurs, and (c) assessment data is used for instructional decision making (Tucker, 1987). Curriculum-based measurement consists of six steps: (a) select appropriate test probes, (b) administer and score the probes, (c) graph the scores, (d) set goals, and (e) communicate progress (Hosp, Hosp, & Howell, 2012).

In addition to frequent monitoring of learner progress and planning to make instructional decisions, CBM is easy to use and is sensitive to student progress and growth over short 10 instructional periods (Burns & Gibbons, 2008). Standardized probes at regular intervals provide progress data that teachers can use to gauge students' growth and establish long-term goals that will lead to proficiency (Fuchs & Fuchs, 2011).

Although probes may differ in that they are based on the curriculum, they measure reading fluency, and consistently with regard to accuracy and automaticity (Roehrig, Nettles, S.M., Hudson, & Torgesen, 2008). The results are graphed so that teachers can easily determine if students meet their reading goals or their educational programs are effective (Fuchs, Fuchs, & Compton, 2004).

Curriculum-based measurement allows comparison of an individual's performance on other similar tasks and to classroom or grade-level peers (Deno, 1985). It can be used as a more individualized approach for making decisions regarding special education eligibility, placement, instruction, and accountability (Mercer, Mercer, & Pullen, 2009). In addition, students are more aware that they are progressing toward a long - term goal, which helps them pay attention to individual learning (McGlinchey & Hixson, 2004)

1.4 Universal Screening

Universal screening is seen as a critical part of any RTI program (Ogonosky, 2008; Ogonosky, 2013; McInerney & Elledge, 2013; Fuchs, Fuchs, & Compton 2012; Smith & Okolo, 2010; Gersten, et al, 2009). It is implemented as part of Tier 1 Intervention with *all* students to identify current and/or potential academic deficits (Smith & Okolo, 2010; Witzel, 2010).

Universal screening instruments may include Curriculum-Based Measures (CBMs), school assessment by RTI team. Some researchers suggest that a single-stage screening may result in a high level of false-positives or false-negatives, unnecessarily increasing a school's investment in RTI or under-identifying students and unacceptably delaying their access to needed interventions. To avoid this challenge, these researchers recommend a two-stage screening, in which the cut point is set sufficiently high so as to eliminate students who clearly are not in need of intervention. This is followed by a second, more detailed assessment of students who did not meet the cut point on the first assessment (Fuchs, Fuchs, & Compton, 2012). Screening measures can be used to assist in determining the effectiveness of curriculum, instruction and interventions provided to students.

1.5   Tiered Instruction

Researchers agree that a tiered system of intervention is critical to an effective RTI system (Ogonosky, 2008; Ogonosky, 2013; McInerney & Elledge, 2013; Fuchs, Fuchs, & Compton 2012). What is often called Tier 1, Level 1, or Primary Intervention is, in essence, regular classroom instruction. Teachers deliver research-based, differentiated instruction to all students (Ogonosky, 2008; McInerney & Elledge, 2013; Fuchs, Fuchs, & Compton 2012; Gersten, et al, 2009).

Based on Universal Screening implemented in Tier 1, students that do not respond adequately to core classroom instruction are moved to Tier 2 Intervention. At this Tier, the intensity of both assessment and instruction intensifies. In Tier 2, significant baseline data collection/diagnostic assessment occurs to pinpoint specific areas in which additional, differentiated, individualized instruction is needed (Ogonosky, 2008; Fuchs, Fuchs, & Compton 2012). As the student progresses through the intervention, curriculum-based and other measures are used frequently to determine whether the student is progressing faster than expected, as expected, or slower than expected compared to clearly-defined student outcome measures. Based on this data, students may be moved back to Tier 1 (general classroom instruction), may remain in Tier 2, or may be moved to Tier 3 for more intensive intervention. Each tiered is below described

1.5.1 Tier 1 Instruction

All students receive high-quality instruction in the general education classroom for 45-90 minutes each day. For example, in mathematics instruction, approximately 70%-85% of all students are expected to respond to instruction provided at this level. A universal screening is administered to identify students who may be struggling with mathematics. After six to ten weeks of subsequent high-quality instruction and progress monitoring, students who continue to struggle as indicated by progress monitoring data receive supplemental instruction at the secondary intervention level.

Hence the general education teacher provides instruction to all students, The instruction is given using whole group instruction, cooperative learning groups, paired instruction and independent practice.

1.5.2 Tier 2 Instruction

Along with their participation in core instruction, students not making adequate progress at the primary instruction level, approximately 10%-20% of the class receives different or additional support. This instruction is provided by the classroom teacher or another educational professional or intervention teachers. This small group instruction is provided to 3-4 students for 30 minutes for 2 days per week. These groups are formed as homogeneous groups. For example, those who struggle in mathematics or reading are grouped with students having same difficulty.

1.5.3 Tier 3 Instruction

A small percentage of students who do not respond to secondary intervention 5%-10% of all students will require even more intensive, individualized instruction (i.e., tertiary intervention). Students receive intensive instruction in small groups of 1-3 students for at least thirty minutes each day. This instruction is typically offered by a specialist in providing and designing individualized interventions.

1.6   Major Components in RTI

1.6.1   Response to Intervention for Reading

The academic area most often targeted in schools that implement response to intervention (RTI) models is beginning reading (Spectrum K12 School Solutions, 2009). Early reading refers to comprehensive school wide frameworks through which students at risk for reading difficulties are identified and provided with evidence-based and data-informed instruction and interventions before they fall alphabet. behind their peers. RTI model addresses early reading difficulties in an effort to provide every student the support necessary to develop adequate reading proficiency.

Multiple studies have demonstrated that with typical instruction, children who do not learn to read adequately in the primary grades will likely continue to struggle with reading in subsequent years (Francis, Shaywitz, Stuebing, Shaywitz, & Fletcher, 1996; Juel, 1988; Torgesen & Burgess, 1998). Stanovich (1986) observed that early difficulties acquiring basic reading skills typically result in limited time engaged in text reading; because of this lack of exposure to text, a relatively mild decoding problem may eventually assume the appearance of a pervasive reading deficit characterized by low fluency, poor vocabulary, and limited world knowledge, all contributing to impaired reading comprehension. By the middle to upper elementary grades, some children have developed reading problems that may cause them to be identified as having learning difficulties primarily because they did not receive appropriate early reading instruction in the primary grades. If the performance gap between typically developing readers and students at risk for reading difficulties is addressed aggressively in the early stages of reading acquisition, more serious reading problems may be prevented. Simmons et al. (2008) observed, "An underlying assumption of RTI is that there is a window of opportunity wherein reading difficulty is more easily altered by instruction and risk of later reading difficulty is likewise minimized". They are multitiered intervention systems in which students are provided with evidence-based classroom reading instruction and supplemental intervention when it is needed, and decisions related to intervention are based on student assessment data.

1.6.2 *Response to Intervention for Early Mathematics*

Professional organizations and educators are striving to reduce the complexity of the early mathematics curriculum. RTI to early mathematics can be straightforward focusing on number sense. Some screening models make only one judgement which may be relative or absolute and this causes decision errors. Curriculum based measurement (CBM) probes of basic (for example, sums to 12, subtraction 0-20 and fact families) and advanced computation skills (finding least common denominator, multidigit multiplication with regrouping, converting numbers to percentages, sllving equations) are empirically supported for screening (VanDerHeyden, Witti, &Naquin, 2003, VanDerHeyden & Witt, 2005). Some Screening models make only judgment (relative or absolute) and this causes decision errors.

These measures have been found to yield reliable scores over time that correlate moderately with other more comprehensive measures of mathematics performance. Research indicates that the use of computation-only assessment and intervention has demonstrated value for early identification of children who are likely to struggle with advanced problem solving in mathematics. Because these probes can be administered to an entire class at one time and require only two minutes of the student's time, they are currently the measures of choice for screening in mathematics.

The areas where many children (25%-50% of those screened) perform poorly indicate the need for system-wide interventions in which all children receive the intervention (i.e., Tier 1). Where small numbers of children perform below the criterion (2-4 students per class), small-or large-group intervention is indicated (i.e., Tier 2). Where only a few children perform poorly (fewer than 1 student per class on average), individualized intervention (i.e., Tier 3) may be immediately planned and implemented for those students. Alternatively, students who fail to respond at Tier 1 or Tier 2 may be provided with a higher level intervention-Tier 2 or Tier 3, respectively.

Following the collection of screening data, the decision team must determine whether a systemic problem exists. Where systemic learning problems are identified, the core program of instruction should be evaluated to ensure that a research-supported curriculum is being used, that instruction is being delivered for sufficient duration and with sufficient quality, and that adequate resources are available to support effective instruction. The adequacy of the core instructional program in mathematics can be evaluated by comparing existing instructional procedures to elements of known effective instructional programs.

1.7 Data-Based Decision Making

An effective RTI system incorporates frequent assessment and progress monitoring at each phase of implementation. However, it is also critical to *use* the data to inform decisions made at multiple points within the intervention process and, conversely, to ensure that every decision made is supported with clear and comprehensive data (Ogonosky, 2008; McInerney & Elledge, 2013; Smith & Okolo, 2010; Gersten, et al, 2009). This is one of the most challenging aspects of RTI to implement with fidelity, as it requires schools to create a clear statement of outcome measures and a comprehensive system of coordinated assessments used to track outcomes over time prior to implementing the intervention system (Ogonosky, 2008). This type of comprehensive framework facilitates the consistent and effective implementation of RTI within and across schools creates a mechanism by which assessment and intervention fidelity can be measured and documented (Ogonosky, 2008; McInerney & Elledge, 2013). In order for data-based decision making to be effective and consistent, it is critical that assessments used be uniform-teacher-to-teacher variations in assessment procedures can undermine the integrity of data used to make decisions about the RTI process and the interventions used (Ogonosky, 2008).

The effectiveness of the intervention was determined on the basis of the progress monitoring data and decisions were made as to which students return to or advance through the instructional tiers. Finally, the RTI team would conclude that a decision of eligibility for special education services.

Regardless of the number of steps in the RTI process, educational decisions periodically required throughout the implementation phase are an integral part of the model. The success of RTI ultimately relies upon the effectiveness of the decision-making process by the RTI team.

1.8   The Role of Special Education

Virtually all students involving implementations of RTI find some struggling readers who fail to respond even to the most intensive levels of intervention (Al Otaiba 2001; Denton, Fletcher, Anthony & Francis, 2006, Denton et al., 2010; Simmons et al., 2011; Speece, Case, & Malloy, 2003; Vellutino & Scanlon 2002. The percentage of non-responders varies across studies depending on variable such as the duration and frequency of interventions, the length of a particular study, and the ages of participants. However, studies such as the preceding ones suggest that, although well-implemented RTI approaches can greatly improve core general education reading instruction and help many struggling readers through prompt interventions, they definitely cannot be expected to address all poor readers' needs successfully. In other words even the best implementation of RTI will not eliminate the need for special education.

Although use of an RTI process may be required for identification of LDs, not all children with disabilities have LDs. Some children, such as those whose disabilities manifest in very early childhood or at birth (Down syndrome, many ASDs, many sensory impairments), will not undergo an RTI process prior to a comprehensive evaluation for special education. Nevertheless, for all students with disabilities, not only LDs, as well as for struggling students in general, RTI approaches can help ensure that children receive good instruction and that the difficulties of children undergoing comprehensive evaluation are not mainly due to inadequate general education practices.

Fuchs, and Stecker (2010) point out that, in the early years of special educators were often the "go-to" experts in a school for general educators seeking help with their most challenging students. However, in recent decades, the identity of special education has weakened, despite the fact that difficult-to-teach students still abound, and schools' records of accomplishment for helping these students - in both general and special education - are not reassuring. Fuchs and collegues (2010) suggest experimental teaching, an approach with a long tradition in special education research (Deno, 1985; Fuchs, Deno & Mirkin, 1984), as an alternative for helping students with the most serious learning difficulties. In this approach, an expert teacher works with students individually or in small groups to implement very intensive intervention, with systematic application of effective teaching strategies, continuous monitoring of children's progress toward benchmarks, data-based decision making, and very frequent, ongoing adjustment of intervention based on the results of progress-monitoring assessment. Experimental teaching indicates many key principles of RTI, applied in a particularly intensive and systematic way.

In the RTI program, special education has an essential role to play in addressing the needs of not only students with identified disabilities but also those who fail to respond to evidence-based interventions implemented in general education, whether or not the children actually meet eligibility criteria for a disability. This role should include serving as expert interventionists as well as consulting and collaborating with general education colleagues and other specialists such as remedial reading teachers, school psychologists, and speech language pathologists. In order to fulfill their roles well, all these specialist groups - and of course, general educators, too - need appropriate preservice preparation and professional development.

1.9   Challenges of Response to Intervention

Screening of entire school populations - with early identification of at-risk readers - is fundamental to all RTI models. Early identification practices must avoid false negatives (truly at-risk students missed by screening) as well as false positives (not at-risk students inappropriately identified for intervention. If schools employ a one-stage universal screen, as appears to be true in most current implementations of RTI, then identifying the majority of truly at-risk students on currently used screening measures involves casting a wide net that will also falsely identify many not-at-risk students (Fuchs, Compton, et al., 2012; Fuchs & Vaughn, 2012; Johnson, Jenkins, Petscher, & Catts, 2009). Furthermore, it appears possible to identify highly at-risk students who should be "fast-tracked" to the most intensive level of intervention (Tier III or special education) rather than being required to demonstrate unresponsiveness in earlier levels first.

Successful implementation of RTI practices requires that both general and special educators have a strong knowledge base about reading.

Although the use of appropriate curricula and programs is very important, meeting the needs of at-risk students in reading requires both research-based methods and knowledgeable teachers (Piasta, Connor, Fishman, & Morrison, 2009). Unfortunately, research on teacher knowledge raises significant concerns about the knowledge base of many elementary level teachers, including special as well as general educators, for implementing RTI. Many teachers appear to lack knowledge, important for effective reading assessment and instruction - and especially for meeting the needs of the most vulnerable readers in a classroom (Brady et al., 2009; Cunningham, Perry, Stanovich & Stanovich, 2004; Moats, 1999 & Poorman 2003; Spear-swerling, Brucker, & Alfano, 2005).

At all grade levels, effective leadership is critical to implementation of RTI because its systematic nature. Among other decisions, those involving screening practices, selection of curricula, purchasing of materials and interventions, and school schedules are ordinarily the purview of the head of the schools and other administrators, not individual teachers. Poor choices in these areas may scuttle RTI efforts before they even begin.

References

1. Al Otaiba (2001). Children who do not respond to early literacy instruction: A longitudinal study across kindergarten and first grade. International Reading Association. Vol.36, No.4, 344-349.
2. Berkeley, S., Bender, W.N, Peaster, L.G, Saunders, L (2009). Implementation of response to intervention: A snapshot of progress. Journal of Learning Disabilities. 42:85-95.
3. Brady, A, et al. (2009) Fault tolerance in protein interaction networks: stable bipartite subgraphs and redundant pathways. *PLoS One* 4(4):e5364
4. Burns, M.K and Gibbons, K.A (2008). *Implementing response-to-intervention in elementary and secondary schools*. Routledge: New York.
5. Cunningham, A.E., Perry, K.E., Stanovich, K.E and Stanovich, P.J (2004). Disciplinary knowledge of K-3 teachers and their knowledge calibration in the domain of early literacy. Annals of Dyslexia, 54, 139-167.
6. Deno, S.L (1985). Curriculum-based Measurement: The emerging alternative. Exceptional Children, 52, 219-232.
7. Deno, S.L (2003). Developments in Curriculum-based Measurement systems for data-based special education problem solving. Focus on Exceptional Children, 19, 1-16.
8. Denton, C.A, Fletcher, J.M, Anthony, J.L and Francis, D.J (2006). An evaluation of intensive intervention for students with persistent reading difficulties. *J Learn Disabil.* 39(5):447-66.
9. Denton, C.A., Nimon, K., Mathes, P.G., Swanson, E.A., Kethley, C., Kurz, T and Shih, M (2010). The effectiveness of a supplemental early reading intervention scaled up in multiple schools. Exceptional Children. 76:394-416.
10. Francis, D.J., Shaywitz, S.E., Stuebing, K.K., Shaywitz, B.A and Fletcher, J.M (1996). Developmental lag verses deficit models of reading disability: A longitudinal, individual growth curves analysis. *Journal of Educational Psychology*, 88, 3-17.

11. Fuchs, D and Fuchs, L.S. (2011). Using CBM for progress monitoring in reading. Washington, DC: National Center on Student Progress Monitoring.

12. Fuchs, D., Compton, D.L, Fuchs, L.S, Hamlett, C.L and Lambert, W (2012). First-grade cognitive abilities as long-term predictors of reading comprehension and disability status. *Journal of Learning Disabilities in press.* 45(3): 217-231.

13. Fuchs, D., Fuchs L.S and Stecker P.M (2010). The "blurring" of special education in a new continuum of general education placements and services. Exceptional Children. 76:301-322.

14. Fuchs, D., Fuchs, L.S and Compton, D.L (2004). Identifying reading disabilities by responsiveness -to-instruction: Specifying measures in criteria. Learning Disability Quarterly, 27, 216-228.

15. Fuchs, D., Fuchs, L.S and Compton, D.L (2012). Smart RTI: A Next-Generation Approach to Multilevel Prevention. Spring; 78(3):263-279.

16. Fuchs, L.S and Vaughn, S. (2012). Responsiveness-to-Intervention: A Decade Later. Journal of Learning Disabilities, 45(3), 195-203.

17. Fuchs, L.S., Deno, S.L and Mirkin, P.K (1984). The effects of frequent curriculum-based measurement and evaluation on pedagogy, student achievement, and student awareness of learning. American Educational Research Journal, 21, 449-460.

18. Gersten, R., Beckmann, S., Clarke, B., Foegen, A., Marsh, L., Star, J. R., & Witzel, B. (2009). Assisting students struggling with mathematics: Response to Intervention (RtI) for elementary and middle schools (NCEE 2009-4060). Washington, DC: National Center for Education Evaluation and Regional Assistance, Institute of Education Sciences, U.S. Department of Education. Retrieved from http://ies.ed.gov/ ncee/wwc/publications/practice guides/.

19. Hosp, K.M., Hosp, J.L and Howell, K. W (2012). A Practical Guide to Curriculum-based Measurement, The Guilford Press, New York, London.

20. Johnson, E.S, Jenkins, J.R, Petscher, Y and Catts, H.W (2009). How can we improve the accuracy of screening instruments? Learning Disabilities Research & Practice. 24:174-185

21. Juel, C. (1988). Learning to read and write: A longitudinal study of 54 children from first through fourth grades. *Journal of Educational Psychology*, 80, 243-255.

22. McGlinchey, M. T., & Hixson, M. D. (2004). Using curriculum-based measurement to predict performance on state assessments in reading. School Psychology Review, 33 (2), 193-203.

23. McInerney, M. & Elledge, A. (2013). Using a response to intervention framework to improve student learning: A pocket guide for state and district leaders. Washington, DC: American Institutes for Research.

24. Mercer, C.D., Mercer, A.R and Pullen, P.C (2009). Teaching Students with Learning Problems, 8th Edition.

25. Moats, L.C (1999). Teaching reading is rocket science. Washington, D.C: American Federation of Teachers.

26. National Research Center on Learning Disabilities. (2003). Information sheet for Regional Resource Centers. Retrieved from http://www.nrcld.org

27. Ogonosky, A (2008). The RTI Guide: Developing and Implementing a Model in Your Schools, John E. McCook, The Response to Intervention Handbook.

28. Ogonosky, A. (2008). The response to intervention handbook: Moving from theory to practice. Austin, TX: Park Place Publications.

29. Ogonosky, A. (2013). RTI: what schools dream for; what schools need. Session presented at D.R.E.A.M: Discovering the Reality of Educating All Minds.

30. Piasta, S.B., Connor, C.M., Fishman, B.J and Morrison, F.J (2009). Teachers' knowledge of literacy concepts, classroom practices, and student reading growth. *Journal of Poverty*, *13*(3), 224-248.

31. Roehrig, A.D, Petscher, Y, Nettles, S.M, Hudson, R.F and Torgesen, J.K (2008). Not just speed reading: Accuracy of the DIBELS oral reading fluency measure for predicting high-stakes

third grade reading comprehension outcomes. Journal of School Psychology. 46:343-366.

32. Simmons, D.C, Coyne, M.D, Kwok, O, McDonagh, S and Harn, B.A (2008). Kame'enui EJ. Indexing response to intervention: A longitudinal study of reading risk from kindergarten through third grade. Journal of Learning Disabilities. 41:158-173

33. Simmons, D.C., Coyne M.D., Hagan-Burke, S., Kwok, O., Johnson, C., Zuo Y and Crevecoeur Y.C (2011). Effects of supplemental reading interventions in authentic contexts: A comparison of kindergarteners' response. Exceptional Children, 77, 207-228.

34. Smith, S. J. & Okolo, C. (2010). Response to intervention and evidence-based practices: Where does technology fit? Learning Disability Quarterly, 33(4), 257-272.

35. Spear S.L and Cheesman, E (2012). Teachers' Knowledge Base for Implementing Response-to-Intervention Models in Reading. *Reading and Writing: An Interdisciplinary Journal*, 25, 7, 1691-1723.

36. Spear-Swerling. L., Brucker, P.O and Alfano, M.P (2005). Teachers' literacy-related knowledge and self-perceptions in relation to preparation and experience. Ann Dyslexia. 55(2):266-96.

37. Speece, D.L., Molloy, D.E and Case, L.P (2003). Starting at the Beginning for Learning Disabilities Identification: Response to Instruction in General Education, in (ed.) Advances in Learning and Behavioral Disabilities (Advances in Learning and Behavioral Disabilities, Emerald Group Publishing Limited, 16, 37 - 50.

38. Stanovich, K.E (1986). Matthew effects in reading: Some consequences of individual differences in the acquisition of literacy. *Reading Research Quarterly, 21,* 360-406.

39. Torgesen, J.K. and Burgess, S.R. (1998). Consistency of reading-related phonological processes throughout early childhood: Evidence from longitudinal, correlational, and instructional studies. In J. Metsala & L. Ehri (Eds.), *Word recognition in beginning reading* (161-188). Hillsdale, N.J.: Erlbaum.

40. Tucker, J. (1987). Curriculum-based assessment is no fad. The Collaborative Educator, 1(4), 4-10.

41. VanDerHeyden, A.M., & Witt, J.C (2005). Quantifying context in assessment: Capturing the effect of base rates on teacher referral and a problem-solving model of identification. School Psychology Review, 34,161-183.

42. VanDerHeyden, A.M., Witt, J.C and Naquin, G. (2003). Development of validation of a process for screening referrals to special education. School Psychology Review, 32, 204-227.

43. VanDerHeyden, A.M., Witt, J.C and Naquin, G. (2003). The development and validation of a process for screening and referrals to special education.

44. Vellutino, F.R and Scanlon, D.M. (2002). The Interactive Strategies approach to reading intervention. Contemporary Educational Psychology, 27, 573-635.

45. Witzel, B.S (2010). Fitting the response to intervention framework with mathematics education. LD Online, http://www.ldonline. org/article/41282/.

2

Response to Intervention in Indian Context

G.Victoria Naomi and Premavathy Vijayan

The Avinashilingam Institute for Home Science and Higher Education for Women has colloborated with the University of Minnesota, Minneapolis, USA in the Indo-US research project titled, "A Sustainable Response to Intervention Model for Successful Inclusion of Children with Disabilities - A India-US Partnership". The Project was about 'Response to Intervention' (RTI) which is a multi-tier approach to the early identification of students struggling academically and support through intervention to accelerate their rate of learning. The primary goal of this project focuses on the development of a sustainable infrastructure within educational systems in India that will allow effective implementation of RTI model and thus enhancing opportunities of inclusion of children with disabilities in the general education classroom.

2.1 Simplified Activity Based Learning (SABL) Curriculum

The Simplified Activity Based Learning curriculum was being followed in all Primary schools in the State of Tamil Nadu. The textbook was integrated with the activity cards. Subject wise learning competencies and targets have been organized into learning units known as milestones or Learning Ladder. Learning ladder concept indicates from the basic concept learning to advanced learning. Students have to complete targeted learning to climb up the next step in the ladder. After analyzing the SABL system, the project team worked out on how RTI model can be integrated into SABL curriculum.

2.2   Selection of Schools for RTI Approach: Rationale

Selection of schools for implementation of the RTI model was done based on similarities of school set up, availability of basic infrastructural facilities, attitude of teachers etc. The RTI project selected two experimental and four control schools for the project. The project has been implemented in the schools for nearly two and half years starting with preparation of Curriculum Based Measurement. The Indian RTI focused the whole school learning approach.

2.3   Preparation of Measurement Tools: Curriculum Based Measurement

The measurement tools have been prepared based on the curriculum of each Grade. This is called Curriculum Based Measurement (CBM). Curriculum-Based Measurement, or CBM, is a method of monitoring student's educational progress through direct assessment of academic skills. CBM can be used to measure basic skills in English Reading and Math Concepts and Computation. While using CBM, the instructor gives the student brief, timed samples, or "probes," made up of academic material taken from the child's school curriculum.

CBM probes are timed and may last from 1 to 5 minutes, depending on the skill being measured. The child's performance on a CBM probe is scored for speed, or fluency, and for accuracy of performance. Since CBM probes are quick to administer and simple to score, they can be given repeatedly for example, twice per week. The results are then charted to offer the instructor a visual record of a targeted child's rate of academic progress.

The close association and interaction with US partner enhanced the knowledge and skills of Indian Team in preparation of CBM probes for English and Math Concepts and Computation. The CBM probes have been prepared using the Computer Assisted Readability Statistics adopted in the USA which is also feasible in Indian context.

2.4 Curriculum Based Measurement for English Reading Probes

The project team prepared different types of English Reading Probes for each Grade Level.

2.4.1 Letter Naming Fluency Probe

Letter naming fluency probes were prepared with 10 rows of random selection of letter with 11 letters in a row making a total of 110 letters in each probe. No letter repeats in its own row or column. Two different list of Letter naming Fluency probes were prepared in this Project.

In the CBM-Letter Name Fluency (LNF) task, the student was given a random list of lower-case letters and had one minute to identify the names of as many letters as possible.

2.4.2 High Frequency Word (HFW) Probe

High Frequency Word Identification Probe was used to monitor students' overall progress in reading at first Grade. HFW was administered individually. The below shown chart presents a sample of HFW probe.

Curriculum-Based Measurement: *Letter Naming Fluency: Grade 1 Probe A*

Student Name & Id: _____ School Name & Id: _____ Date:_____

a	j	h	m	t	n	z	o	k	x	f	/11(11)
p	v	s	e	r	d	y	c	q	u	w	/11(22)
g	l	b	i	k	a	m	i	q	l	n	/11(33)
d	j	p	x	w	r	y	f	g	e	h	/11(44)
c	s	t	z	o	u	v	b	d	s	l	/11(55)
o	x	u	e	i	n	b	t	z	w	f	/11(66)
m	j	h	v	k	q	a	p	r	g	y	/11(77)
c	w	r	z	q	x	m	f	d	h	k	/11(88)
a	l	v	i	b	p	n	c	e	t	y	/11(99)
g	u	j	s	o	x	a	s	i	u	e	/11(110)

#/Correct: _____ #/Errors: _____

CBM : High-Frequency Word Identification: Grade 1, Probe A

Student Name & Id: _____ School Name & Id: _____ Date:_____

stop	give	as	an	4/4
just	take	old	thank	4/8
round	live	had	some	4/12
over	let	put	could	4/16
every	her	going	from	4/20
once	him	any	where	4/24
ask	think	after	has	4/28
of	by	know	again	4/32

Correct Items:_____ Total Items Attempted:_____

The examiner presents the student with a single page with 110 words. The 110 words have been chosen from the Dolch 100 most frequent words list which is relevant to the beginners (The Dolch Word List, was compiled by Edward William Dolch, 1948).

The student has one minute time to read the words. The assesser marks student's errors on a separate score sheet. The score is calculated by counting the number of correct words read in 1 minute.

2.4.3 Oral Reading Fluency (ORF) Probe

Reading passages for English Oral Reading Fluency have been developed for Grade I to V. Readability Statistics measure was used while preparing the passage. Readability statistics measure text features that are subject to mathematical calculations such as number of syllables and sentence length for reading ease and reading Grade level.

Readability Statistics	? X
Counts	
Words	108
Characters	416
Paragraphs	1
Sentences	14
Averages	
Sentences per Paragraph	14.0
Words per Sentence	7.7
Characters per Word	3.6
Readability	
Passive Sentences	7%
Flesch Reading Ease	98.7
Flesch-Kincaid Grade Level	1.4
	OK

Example of Readability statistics for Grade 1 is shown here for a selected passage.

The statistics show the features of the passage and the reading Grade Level is 1.4 indicating that the selected passage is appropriate for the I Grade children. Using the formulae, passages for Oral Reading Fluency for all Grades were prepared. The Oral reading fluency passages have been prepared collecting 30% of vocabularies from the first term, 40% from 2nd term and 30% from the final and the third term portions of the curriculum.

2.4.4 *English Reading Passage with Maze*

Curriculum-Based Measurement for reading using reading passage with maze is a tool ideally suited to assess student reading comprehension (Parker, Hasbrouck & Tindal, 1992). The student is given a specially formatted sample of text. The first sentence of the Maze passage is left intact. In the remainder of the passage, every seventh word is selected to be incorporated into a response item that consists of the original word plus two foils (words that would not make sense if substituted in the passage in place of the original, correct word). These three choices are randomly arranged and inserted back into the text. When reading the Maze passage, the reader reviews each response item and circles the word from the three choices that best restores the meaning of that segment of the passage. Two CBM maze passages have been developed for each Grade level from Grade III - V. A sample maze passage for Grade IV is given below for reference.

4 Maze English   Student Name: _____

Level 4 Passage A
Runa and the Wise Man

There was a girl who lived in a small town in Tamil Nadu. Her name was Runa. Runa (**went/drank/pool**) to an elementary school near her (**journey/house/salt**). That week the class was (**cooking/learning/opening**) about the many cultures and religions in (**India/ /road/onion**).They learnt that differences among people **pollute/smile/make** India a wonderful country. People can (**skip/learn/paint**) from one another. There are Hindus, Muslims, Sikhs, Buddhists, Jains, Parsees, Christians, and Jews. Each (**book/religion/scarf**) has its own places where (**people/paper/wells**) can gather and pay respects. Hindus, Buddhists, Jains and Parsees (**water/gather/repair**) at their Temples. Sikhs gather at Gurudwaras. Christians (**like/sow/go**) to Church and Jews gather at a Synagogue.

Runa (**bee/was/caught**) listening very carefully to the (**teacher/church/cloud**). She was puzzled. She had (**pretty/many/calm**) questions. She wondered why people (**ate/toss/met**) different foods and wore different (**kinds/trends/woods**) of clothes. She wanted to know (**for/why/shy**) they answered her questions in different (**key/sways/size**). One day, she was walking by a (**big/cry/cold**)tree in her town. There was a (**blue/wall/wise**) man sitting there very calmly. Runa (**opened/asked/fetched**) the wise man, "Why do people (**gather/sell/grow**) in different buildings when they want (**pay/hurry/ omit**) their respects?" "Why don't they all (**leap/go/slow**) a Temple, a Church or a (**parrot/synagogue/orphanage**)? "Is there anything magical about the (**places/lions/trees**)?"

The below table shows the number of reading passages developed for English Reading.

Development of Reading Passages

S.No	Grade	Curriculum Based Measurement (Test Item)	No Probes	Test completion Time
1.	I	Letter Naming Fluency	2	1 mt each
		High Frequency Word Identification	2	1 mt each
		Oral Reading Fluency Passage	2	1 mt each
2.	II	Oral Reading Fluency Passage	2	1 mt each
3.	III	Oral Reading Fluency Passage	2	1 mt each
		Maze Passages	2	3 mt each
4.	IV	Oral Reading Fluency Passage	2	1 mt each
		Maze Passage	2	3 mt each
5.	V	Oral Reading Fluency Passage	2	1 mt each
		Maze Passage	2	3 mt each
Total Probes			**20 Probes**	

2.5 Curriculum Based Measurement for Mathematics

CBM mathematics measures provide information on whether students are on track to meet performance goals, whether instruction is effective for students, and whether instructional modifications are necessary.

In primary school, both computation and concepts and applications measures are being used. Computation measures include single or mixed basic facts or multi-step addition, subtraction, multiplication, or division problems. Concepts and applications measures include problems that ask students to apply their mathematics knowledge, including problems that address concepts such as greater than/less than, measurement, money, and temperature.

2.5.1 Curriculum Based Measurement for Math Concept & Application

The aim of measurement is to develop Math Concept & Application and is described as an approach that "systematically samples the year-long curriculum so that each skill is represented and receives the same emphasis on each alternate forum". Using this approach, math concept probes have been developed. In each Math Concept probe, the project team developed 15 items for instance concept of place value, fraction, angles etc. Examples of I Grade Math Concept Probes are given below:

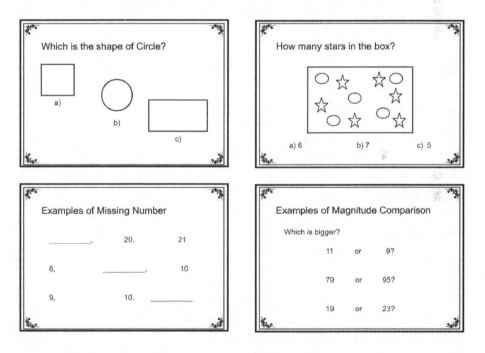

The table below presents the number of probes prepared and administered among students in respective Grade.

Development of Math Probes

S.No	Grade	Curriculum Based Measurement (Test Item)	No Probes	Test Completion Time
1.	I	Math Concept & Application	1	3 mt
2.	II	Math Concept & Application	2	3 mt each
3.	III	Math Concept & Application	2	3 mt each
4.	IV	Math Concept & Application	2	3 mt each
5.	V	Math Concept & Application	2	3 mt each
Total Probes			**9 Probes**	

2.5.2 *Curriculum Based Measurement for Math Computation*

The Math Computation probes include 2 tests at each Grade level for Grades 1-5. Each test consists of 30 math computation problems representing the year-long, Grade-level Math computation curriculum selected 30% from first term, 40% mid term and 30% from third term curriculum of each Grade. The type of problems represented on each test remains constant from test to test. For example, at Grade 3, each Computation test includes five

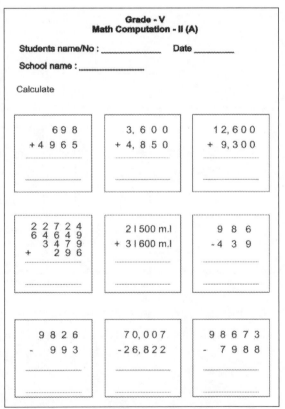

multiplication facts with factors zero through five and four multiplication facts with factors six through nine. However, the facts to be tested and their positions on the tests have been selected randomly. CBM Computation can be administered to a group of students at one time. The administrator presents each student with a CBM Computation test. Students have a set amount of time to answer the math problems on the Computation test. Timing the CBM Computation test correctly is critical to ensure consistency from test to test. The administrator times the students during the test and scores the tests later. Student performance on the Computation test is scored as the total number of digits correct.

Math Computation Probe Developed for Administration of Test

S. No	Grade	Curriculum Based Measurement (Test Item)	Probes Administered	Time for completion
1.	I	Math Computation	1	3 mt
2.	II	Math Computation	2	3 mt each
3.	III	Math Computation	2	3 mt each
4.	IV	Math Computation	2	3 mt each
5.	V	Math Computation	2	3 mt each
Total Probes			**9 Probes**	

2.6 Curriculum Based Measurement for Tamil Reading (Tamil: Regional Language)

Curriculum Based measurement passages for Tamil reading was prepared for Grade I to V. Vocabularies from the curriculum of each Grade were sorted and probes were developed. Probes have been developed collecting vocabularies from the I, II and III term lessons with the percentage of 30%, 40% and 30% of the portions respectively.

The passages have been prepared in line with the characteristics of words similar to English words getting approximation of readability statistics as per Flesch formulae for English (e.g number of words, character, sentence, passive sentences etc).

Details of Tamil Probes Prepared

S. No	Grade	Curriculum Based Measurement (Test Item)	Probes Administered	Test completion Time
1.	I	Letter Naming Fluency	2	1 mt each
		High Frequency Word	2	1 mt each
		Oral Reading Fluency Passage	2	1 mt each
2.	II	Oral Reading Fluency Passage	2	1 mt each
		Maze Passage	2	3 mt each
3.	III	Oral Reading Fluency Passage	2	1 mt each
		Maze Passage	2	3 mt each
4.	IV	Oral Reading Fluency Passage	2	1 mt each
		Maze Passage	2	3 mt each
5	V	Oral Reading Fluency Passage	2	1 mt each
		Maze Passage	2	3 mt each
		Total Probes	**22 probes**	

2.7 Validation of Curriculum Based Measurement (Pre-Pilot Data Collection)

For establishing reliability and validity of the probes, pre pilot data collection has been undertaken in two schools with 80 sample, 10 sample from each Grade from I to IV in each school. The probes were found to be both reliable and valid. The layout below shows the inter-rater reliability of the test administrators.

The curriculum Based measurement has been administered by Research and Project Assistants. Inter-rater reliability has been established before administering the tests to the total sample. The following table shows the result.

Reliability Score of the Data Collectors

S.No	Reliability Between Test Administrators	Test Items	Reliability Score
1.	Between two Research Assistants	English ORF	90%
2.	Between two Research Assistants	Math Probes	90%
3.	Between two Research Assistants and two Project Assistants	English ORF	95%
4.	Between two Research Assistants and two Project Assistants	Math Probes	98%

2.8 Administering & Scoring Reading Probes

The examiner and the student sit across the table from each other. There are two copies of the same probe for teacher and the student. In the teacher's copy, each word in a sentence is counted and the total number of words in each sentence is noted at the end of each sentence. Teacher's copy helps the teacher to score easily. The examiner hands over the student the unnumbered copy of the CBM reading probe. The examiner takes the numbered copy of the passage, shielding it from the student's view. Below shown are samples.

Student Name & Id :_____School Name & Id: _____Date:_____

Level 3: Passage A
Teachers Copy
The Queen, Her Sons, and the Tiger

Once there was a wise queen. She had two sons who she loved very much. The queen	17
dreamed that one day each son would develop the wisdom to rule the kingdom.	31
Springtime came and the kingdom was in trouble. A huge tiger from the jungle was eating	47
the farm animals, and frightening the farmers. They would not go out to tend their crops	63
People had little food to eat. The queen called her sons and took each to a room in the	82
palace. She said, our people need food. Use your talents and fill this room with anything	98
you wish so that our people can eat. It can be anything!	110
One week later, the queen excitedly went to the oldest son's room. It was completely	125
filled with rice. Her son bought the rice from a merchant with precious gold coins. The	141
queen was not satisfied. She was ashamed of her son. The rice would quickly be eaten.	157
The people would be hungry once again.	164
The queen then went to the entrance of the room of her younger son. He grabbed his	181
mother and dragged her into the room. It was completely dark. She could see nothing.	196

	Total Words Read	
	Errors	
	Total Words Read Correctly	

Comprehension questions
Score "1" for a correct answer and "0" for an incorrect answer:

1. How many sons were for the queen?	
2. What kind of animal was eating chickens and goats and frightening the farmers?	
3. What did the oldest son fill his room with?	
4. With what did the youngest son reward the tiger?	
Total	

32

Level 3: Passage A
The Queen, Her Sons, and the Tiger

Student Copy

Once there was a wise queen. She had two sons who she loved very much. The queen dreamed that one day each son would develop the wisdom to rule the kingdom.

Springtime came and the kingdom was in trouble. A huge tiger from the jungle was eating the farm animals, and frightening the farmers. They would not go out to tend their crops People had little food to eat. The queen called her sons and took each to a room in the palace. She said, our people need food. Use your talents and fill this room with anything you wish so that our people can eat. It can be anything!

One week later, the queen excitedly went to the oldest son's room. It was completely filled with rice. Her son bought the rice from a merchant with precious gold coins. The queen was not satisfied. She was ashamed of her son. The rice would quickly be eaten. The people would be hungry once again.

The queen then went to the entrance of the room of her younger son. He grabbed his mother and dragged her into the room. It was completely dark. She could see nothing.

The examiner says to the student: *"When I say, 'start,' begin reading aloud at the top of this page. Read across the page* [demonstrate by pointing]. *Try to read each word. If you come to a word you don't know, I'll tell it to you. Be sure to do your best reading. Are there any questions?* [Pause] *Start"*

The examiner begins the stopwatch when the student says the first word. If the student does not say the initial word within 3 seconds, the examiner says the word and starts the stopwatch. As the student reads along in the text, the examiner records any errors by marking a slash (/) through the incorrectly read word. If the student hesitates for 3 seconds on any word, the examiner says that word and marks it as an error. At the end of 1 minute, the examiner says, *Stop* and marks the student's concluding place in the text with a bracket (]). Reading fluency is calculated by first determining the total words attempted within the timed reading probe and then deducting from that total the number of incorrectly read words.

This procedure was followed in 'Letter Naming Fluency', 'Frequency Word Identification' and 'Oral Reading Fluency' Probes for both English and Tamil reading.

2.9   Administering & Scoring of CBM Maze Probes

1. The examiner split the Grade level students into 20 in a group.
2. The examiner distributes copies of CBM Maze probes A & B alternatively to all the students in the group.
3. The examiner says: "When I say 'begin', start reading the story silently. Wherever you come to a group of 3 word-choices, circle the word that makes sense. Work as fast as you can but do your best work. If you finish the first page, go to the next page and continue working until I tell you to stop."
4. The examiner says: "Ready? Begin" and starts the stopwatch.
5. After 3 minutes, the examiner stops the stopwatch and says: "Stop. Pencils/Pens down".
6. These directions are repeated for each Maze passage administered in a session. The examiner then collects and scores the passages.

2.10 Administering & Scoring CBM Math Probes for Concept & Application - Individual Measure

In the research project, probes for Math Concept & Application were administered to individuals in I Grade. For Grade II - V, each student takes test on his/her own. But for the Grade 1 students who were the beginners, who were not able to read the probes tests have been conducted with the help of the assesser/ examiner.

2.10.1 Instruction to the Examiner before Test

1. Administer the probe and say the direction individually.
2. Place the sample flash card booklet with sample problems before the students.

The examiner can say,

> *Look at the sheet before you. There will be a question with three choices of answers. Show the question and three choices to the student.*
>
> *Ask the student to show the three choices again. Make sure that the student understands about the three choices with examples.*
>
> *In the three choices one answer is correct.*
>
> *I will read you the question you have to show me the one correct answer.*
>
> *If you do not know answer you will move on to next question.*
>
> **Demonstrate: Read the question and ask the child to show the correct answer.**
>
> *When I say next, you turn the next sheet. Then I will read the next question.*
>
> **Demonstrate: Make the student to turn the next sheet on his/her own.**
>
> *Do you understand the process? Any questions?*

2.10.2 Instruction during Test

1. Keep the scoring sheet with student name & ID and place the flash card booklet before the student.
2. Start the stop watch and read the first question. If the student fails to show the answer in 5 sec after reading the question mark, an 'X' near in the question in the scoring sheet and move on to next question.
3. End of the 3 minutes stop the stop watch and say 'Thank you'

4. If the student has gone through all the questions before three minutes, note the time in his/her scoring sheet.
5. If the student makes three consecutive errors or skips, then stop administering the test.
6. Count down the number of correct answers and number of questions attended.

2.11 Administering & Scoring Math Concept & Application - Group Measure

CBM Concepts and Applications can be administered to a group of students at one time. The administrator presents each student with a CBM Concept and Application test. Students have a set 3 minutes of time to answer the math problems on the test, 3 minutes each for Math Concepts and Math Computation. Timing the CBM Concepts and Applications test correctly is critical to ensure consistency from test to test. The administrator times the students during the test and scores the tests later.

2.11.1 Instruction to the Assesser before the Test

1. Place the Cover Sheet with sample math questions before the students.
2. Explain the sample problems to the group of students with the black board.

The examiner can say,

> Look at the sheet before you there will be a question with three choices of answers.

> Read the question and the three choices. Now say which is the correct answer from the three choices.

> Tick the correct answer with your pencil.

You need not write the correct answer in any place.

Do you understand the process correctly? Any questions?

We are going to answer math questions for 3 minutes. I will give you the question paper with some math questions that you have to answer in the same manner.

Be ready with your pencil."When I say 'begin', start reading the questions and tick the correct answer"

If you do not know the correct answer do not worry mark an 'X' near the question and move on to the next question.

You may know the answer for many questions so do not stick on to the same question which you do not know the answer.

If you finish the first page turn the page and continue working until I say 'Thank you'

Do your best.

'When I say 'Thank you' stop working and put down your pencils/Pens.

Are you clear? Any questions.

2.11.2 Instruction during Test

1. Place the probe before the student and say "Begin" and start the stop watch.
2. If some student finishes before the time limit, note the time they have taken.
3. At the end of 3 minute say 'Thank you'
4. Collect the probes and score them.

Student's performance is scored as the total number of blanks correct and one score for each correct answer. The examiner stops scoring when there is three consecutive errors or skips in the probes. The examiner totals the number of questions answered correctly and also total the number items answered by the each student in each probe.

2.12 Administering & Scoring Math Computation - Group Measure

Group measures are administered by splitting the group in to two - minimum of 20 students in a group for Grade of 40 students.

2.12.1 Instruction to the Examiner before the Test

1. For 1 and 2 Grades give a sample probe sheet so that they could see the problems. For other Grades explain using black board.
    We are going to do 3 minutes math test.
    I will give you the question paper with some problems. (Addition, Subtraction, Multiplication, Division) - show the probe sheet.

2. Explain the sample problems to the group of students with the black board. (Addition, Subtraction, Multiplication, Division)
    Be ready with your pencil. When I say 'Begin' start answering the problems. Look at each problem carefully before you answer it. Begin with the first problem and work across the page (point). Then go to the next row.
    If you cannot answer the problem mark an 'X' through it and try to answer the next problem. (Demonstrate using black board, For 1 & 2 std make the student to mark 'X' on their sample probe sheet)
    If you finish a page, turn the next page (Demonstrate using black board, for 1 & 2 Grade make them to turn the next page of their sample probe sheet)and continue working until I say 'Thank you'.

When I say 'Thank you'. Then put down your pencils and stop working. Say' Begin' and start the stop watch. At the end of 3 minutes say: 'Thank you'

3. If any student finishes before the time limit of 3 minutes, note the time on their probe.
   Collect & Score the probes.

When scoring CBM Computation, students receive one(1) score for each correctly answered digit. The number of correct digits within the set time limit is the student's score. Scoring each digit correct in the answer is a more sensitive index of student change so that typically evaluated by the overall student growth or deterioration earlier can be evaluating correct digits in the answers.

2.13 Universal Screening: Indian Schools

Universal screening is the first step in identifying the students who are at risk for learning difficulties. It is the mechanism for targeting students who struggle to learn when provided a scientific, evidence-based general education (Jenkins, Hudson & Johnson, 2007). Universal screening is typically conducted three times per school year, beginning of the term, middle and end of the term. Universal screening measures are CBM measures on target skills (e.g., phonological awareness in English, Math concept and computation skills etc.) that are highly predictive of future outcomes.

In the Indian RTI model, all students both in Experimental and Control Groups were screened in English reading, awareness of Math Concept and Math computation in order to provide intervention in the at- risk area. Identification of risk area helps prevention services before the onset of substantial academic deficits. The goal of early identification of potential problems is to increase the likelihood of at-risk students developing adequate academic competence. The screening measures (CBM measures) prepared for the project has the following four Psychometric properties which will increase the likelihood of true positives and decrease the likelihood of false positives.

Sensitivity: It is the degree to which a screening mechanism reliably identifies at-risk students who, in fact, perform unsatisfactorily. A screening measure with good sensitivity helps reduce the numbers of false negatives.

Specificity: The screening measures identify students who later perform satisfactorily on a criterion measure. A screening measure with good specificity also helps reduce the numbers of false positives. This is critical in an RTI model because false positives lead to a waste of time and money, and may result in inappropriate instruction for students who do not need it. The measures developed had with specificity.

Practicality: An effective screening measure should also be brief and simple. An efficient screening measure will quickly identify students who are lagging behind their peers, thereby maximizing instructional time. A simple screening measure does not require a specialist like school psychologist or a special educator for administration and can be performed in the classroom. This may help reducing student's test anxiety and results can be computed and interpreted in a quick and efficient manner. The reading passages will be administered in one minute and math probes for three minutes. All these qualities were borne in mind while developing the measures.

Consequential Validity: Effective universal screening measures should also be consequentially valid. This means the screening measure does no harm to the student and is linked to effective interventions.

2.14 Universal Screening

2.14.1 Data Collection Procedure in the Selected Indian Schools

Data collection was carried out alternatively in the two experimental schools. It helped avoiding artificial differences of scores due to differences in length of days in collecting data in one school or other. Data collection was carried out in all the schools within the stipulated data collection window period i.e maximum of 15 days with 10 data collectors.

2.14.2 Grouping Students for Intervention in the Project

Based on the universal screening scores, students were grouped for intervention. The first phase of universal screening indicated that a majority (90%) of students was below 25th percentile and hence all students were placed under Tier II intervention for a period of 3 months. After a 3 month intervention, the next universal screening was administered, and based on scores, students were regrouped for Tiered instructions.

Grade	Subject	2015		
		Tier 1	*Tier 2*	*Tier 3*
3	English	56%	27%	17%
	Tamil	65%	20%	16%
	Math	57%	26%	17%
4	English	55%	29%	16%
	Tamil	68%	19%	14%
	Math	62%	23%	15%
5	English	62%	24%	14%
	Tamil	67%	18%	15%
	Math	62%	24%	14%

The above table indicates that students in Tier 2 and Tier 3 needed intervention. It is also revealed that almost 50% of the students required intervention when RTI model was introduced.

2.15 Tiered Instruction

Response to Intervention (RTI) is a process to identify students at risk and provide targeted teaching to help academically struggling students. The progress of all students measured three times in a year with validated tools. The three tiered instruction addresses every child's needs. The amount of extra helps increases with each Tier from Tier I to Tier 3.

2.15.1 Tier 1: The Whole Class

Regular Class room teachers were trained to use a variety of supports as soon as student begins to struggle such as re-teaching, differentiated instruction, and/or additional practice. Within Tier 1, all students received scientifically based instruction provided by the trained teachers to ensure that students' difficulties are not due to inadequate instruction. As stated, the entire class was screened three times a year to identify students who were at risk of failing. All students' progress was tracked using the validated measurement tools. Students who were not showing adequate progress in the regular class room instruction were move to Tier 2 instruction.

2.15.2 Tier 2: Small Group Interventions

When the students in Tier 1 is not making adequate progress, he/she will get instructions in a small group two or three times a week. In the project the instruction was provided by the intervention teachers and they were the Research/Project Assistants in the project. In Tier 2, there were 6-8 students who received interventions for 30 minutes for two times a week. The intervention teachers were trained to provide minute to minute engagement of students in the small group.

Their skills were assessed every other week to monitor the student's progress and decision making.

2.15.3 Tier 3: Intensive Interventions

If the student's score is below 25th percentile and not making adequate progress in Tier 2, he/she will receive more intensive instruction in specific skills. There were 5-6 students in the Tier 3 in Indian RTI model. The intervention teachers provided 3 times instruction mostly individualized in a week with 30 minutes each session. The progress of the students were monitored every week and after 6 weeks progress monitoring data, if the student was not showing any progress, the student was referred for special education services.

The students were intervened for enhancement of reading and math ability on four cycles. Each cycle had duration of 3 or 4 months.

2.16 Progress Monitoring and Data Based Decision Making

Progress monitoring is used to assess students' academic performance, to quantify a student rate of improvement or responsiveness to instruction, and to evaluate the effectiveness of instruction. Progress monitoring was implemented to students in Tier 2 and Tier 3.

Progress monitoring is a critical factor in the RTI project. The Progress monitoring was being held for Tier II Students once in two weeks i.e 15th day during Intervention and Tier III Students after every week of intervention i.e 8th day during Intervention for English Reading, Tamil Reading and Math ability. Set of Progress monitoring reading probes were developed based on the curriculum. And student's scores were recorded and analyzed for progress and decision making for academic growth. After 6 data point, progress of the students was analyzed and decision was taken to change Tiers or place students if they fit to be in Tier I instruction.

From Jan 2015 to March 2016, there were 14 Progress monitoring to Tier III students and 11 progress monitoring for Tier II students.

2.17 Data Meeting

Data meeting is an integral part of RTI model. Student's progress monitoring scores were discussed with regular classroom teacher to determine the level of the student and intervention efficacy in terms of academic achievement.

RTI grade-level Data meeting include the principal, all teachers from that grade level, the intervention teachers, and the data manager i.e the individual who manages benchmark and progress-monitoring data.

The RTI team arranges for meeting logistics, such as scheduling, and the school principal often acts as facilitator of the meeting. Data Meeting should be conducted after minimum each universal screening i.e typically three times per year.

Prior to meetings, the data should be compiled and sent to all team members ahead of time in a user-friendly format so that all team members can review the data to familiarize themselves with it before the meeting. Data shared with the team can include results of measures such as universal screening and progress monitoring scores using both raw data and visual displays (e.g., graphs and histograms) of individual and group data.

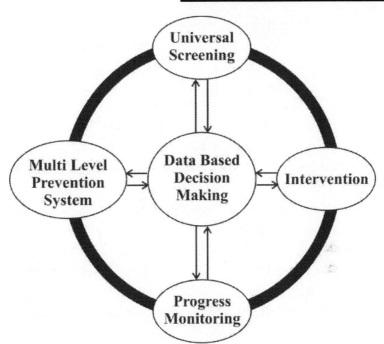

2.17.1 Tier 1 Analysis

At First, the team should review whole-grade performance on the universal screening conducted for that grade level. The team should review what percentage of students is at each performance/risk level: Next, the team uses the percentages at each level to set measurable goals to achieve by the next review point. The goals should be stated in terms of the percentage of students making a particular amount of progress toward the identified benchmark.

After reviewing the students' current performance and setting goals for the next universal screening, the team lists whole-class instructional strategies to consider implementing to improve student performance. Ideas should be recorded in a list that is easily viewed by everyone. The team analyzes and rates the listed strategies according to the extent to which they are evidence based, practical, and available or according to the feasibility of their creation. Finally, the team selects which strategies to implement during the next intervention period.

2.17.2 Tier 2 Analysis

The team now identifies which students will be considered for Tier 2 interventions. Students meeting criteria for Tier 2 services are identified based on their risk level for academic difficulties as indicated by benchmark scores. More specifically, students whose performance is in the emerging or strategic range of the data sets are identified. All available data on these students are reviewed, such as universal screening scores and progress-monitoring data. In reviewing each student's data, all areas of assessment should be considered to determine what kind of learning profile the student has and to ensure that the assessments validate each other. Based on all of this information, the team decides which students need Tier 2 interventions. For each of the identified students, the team sets a measurable goal in terms of specified benchmark scores for the next review point. The team now focuses on tiered intervention strategies. Based on students' needs in Tier 2, the team determines which strategies apply.

2.17.3 Tier 3 Analysis

Next, the team focuses on identifying students and planning interventions for Tier 3. Students chosen for Tier 3 are typically those performing the lowest on universal screenings. Because these students need the most intensive supports, however, planning for specific interventions according to need may be more involved than Tier 2 planning. For instance, a closer look at progress-monitoring data may be necessary to make decisions for students in Tier 3. Students who continue to display deficits in level and rate of improvement after Tier 3 supports may be referred to the special education evaluation process.

Reference

1. Edward William Dolch (1948). Problems in Reading: Original from the University of Michigan, Publisher Garrard Press, P.373.
2. Parker, R., Hasbrouck, J.E., & Tindal, G. (1992). The maze as a classroom-based reading measure: Construction methods, reliability, and validity. *Journal of Special Education*, Vol.*26*, Pp.195-218.

Teaching English Reading through Response to Intervention

R.Shanthi and M.Revathi

Many children enjoy reading. But for some, it is a painful process. Every child with average intelligence who lacks reading skills will develop the appropriate reading skills if taught by a teacher or parent who has the "know how" to teach the child. Every child who experiences difficulty in reading is entitled to be initiated into a programme in which he/she will be respected and trained to achieve the necessary skills. In an inclusive set up the child encounters difficulty in reading due to various reasons.

It could be

- Learning difficulty - (Students who lack intellectual ability).

- Specific Learning difficulty (Dyslexia - or difficulty with language).

- English as a second language Instruction.

- Difficulty in encoding & decoding the letters of the alphabet.

- Difficulty in visualizing visuals.

Ability to read depends on the child's knowledge of the letters, its name and sound. Every word has a sequence of letters. The child should be able to remember and identify the form of words. This child should have the knowledge of Alphabetic Principle and Phonemic

Awareness. In short, development of encoding and decoding skill is of prime importance in developing reading skills.

In English we have two groups of words - Phonetic or Auditory words and Visual or Non-Phonetic words. To read a text, a child needs Print Awareness. A page contains organised printed matter. It needs to be read from left to right. Every word has space in between. Each sentence begins with a capital letter and the sentence ends with a full stop.

Rani is given a small passage by her teacher to read. This is how she reads.

"I bull beg it mad

I me but"

But the correct reading is:

"I have a blue boat. It is big. It is made of wood. I like my boat.

The letters of the alphabet form the words. So the initial step in teaching the child is to teach him the sounds of the alphabet. The child needs to learn to chant the letters in the proper order. He needs to know and distinguish the sounds of the consonants and vowels. Short vowels and long vowels need to be reinforced effectively. The child needs to see the letter, know its name and the sound the letter makes.

3.1 Phases of Reading development in typically Developing Children

Phase	Key features	Approximate grades
Visual-cue (prealphabetic) word recognition	Little grasp of alphabetic principle; use mainly of visual cues in word recognition; limited letter knowledge and phonological awareness	Pre-kindergarten
Phonetic-cue (partial alphabetic) word recognition	Grasp of alphabetic principle; some use of phonetic cues to recognize words; more advanced levels of letter knowledge and phonological awareness than in previous phase; reading comprehension far below listening level	Kindergarten to about middle of first grade
Controlled (full alphabetic) word recognition	Full use of phonetic cues in word recognition; full phonemic awareness; word recognition of common words is generally accurate but not highly automatic; decoding of unusual, complex, or multisyllabic words still limited; reading comprehension still well below listening level	Later first grade to second grade
Automatic (consolidated alphabetic) word recognition	Recognition of common words quickly and effortlessly as well as accurately; better reading of multisyllabic words; automatic word reading integrated with comprehension processes for fluent text reading at grade level; reading still below listening level	Later second grade to third grade
Strategic reading	Increasing morphological knowledge and awareness; increasing ability to read complex or unusual words; highly accurate, automatic recognition of most words, with fluent text reading at grade level; routine use of at least some strategies to aid comprehension; reading used as a tool for gathering information; gap between reading comprehension and listening comprehension starting to close	About third grade to sixth grade
Proficient reading	Increasing higher order comprehension abilities, with the ability to read critically as well as evaluate and integrate information across multiple sources; highly accurate, automatic recognition of most words, with fluent text reading at grade level; reading comprehension comparable to listening comprehension and may even exceed listening for certain types of texts	About seventh grade to eighth grade through adulthood

This displays only a few examples of relevant Common Core State Standards (CCSS); to see the full set of K-12 English Language Arts standards, go to http://www.corestandards.or_g/ELA-Literacy/RH/ introduction. *Source:* Spear-Swerling (2004a).

3.2 English Teaching in Indian Schools

There is no argument against the fact that English teaching in Indian schools is traditional in methodology and teaching learning procedures of the language teachers are outdated. Many, if not all, schools have continued with the conventional methods. In many schools teachers transmit the lessons by self-reading, explaining, discussing without giving learners opportunity to make inferences of their own appreciation.

As Second language, English was taught by the teachers like other subjects like science, social studies, mathematics and had very little opportunity to use it functionally.

Many teachers in the United States are faced with the challenge of teaching children to read and write in English when the students have a heritage language that is not English and they are not yet proficient in English. Making this a more critical issue, several studies (North Central Regional Educational Laboratory, 2003; Southeast Center for Quality Teaching, 2003) suggest that teachers are not receiving adequate professional development in effective strategies to address the English learners' literacy development. Thompson (2004), in a recent Special Report that reviewed the current research related to quality literacy instruction for English learners, concludes that classroom teachers urgently need to know more about effective strategies for teaching English learners. As part of the effort to learn more about quality instruction for English learners, educational researchers and teachers in the United States have looked at instructional practices in other countries. When those countries are faced with the same challenge of teaching children in English to learn to read and write in English, there has been greatest transfer of best practices (Clay, 1991; Holdaway, 1978; Frater & Standiland, 1994). Research and close observation of the teaching of reading has been conducted in Australia and New Zealand, and a smaller amount of study in England for the obvious reason that

English is the language of instruction. Literacy instruction in India has not received the same attention, perhaps because English is not the first language of the majority. There are studies that compare and contrast educational practices in India to those in the United States with respect to the goals that teachers have for student learning, the way teachers approach the curriculum and the textbook, the way knowledge is communicated to students, and the way teachers interact verbally with their students (Clark, 2001; Alexander, 2000). There is however, very little literature that reveals current methods and practice in Indian primary classrooms for the teaching of reading to children whose first language is not English.

3.3 Major Language Learning Barriers

Despite the fact that Indian schools are now well equipped with English teaching-learning techniques like audio-visual material, digital tools, besides qualified teachers, the level and standard of English teaching-learning in many reputed schools is abysmal. Some of the barriers are:

3.3.1 Excessive Use of Mother Language

Though the use of mother tongue in teaching second language helps a child to get inferences to incorporate into targeted language, but excessive use of mother tongue tends to curb the naturalness of the process of learning a new language. The teachers or parents while teaching the second language to the child translate the word to regional language. This limits the scope of acquiring and learning of English faster and better.

3.3.2 Lack of Oral Communication

In many English medium schools teachers as well as students lag behind in oral communication. Before starting a lesson, teachers rarely engage learners in warm up activities. Direct teaching by teachers makes students passive listeners. Sometimes teachers do not teach for language development rather they focus on the examination the child has to qualify after completing a course or unit.

3.3.3 Lack of Grammar Integration in the Learning Process

Regardless of the country or the language, grammar is the foundation for communication — the better the grammar, the clearer the message, the more likelihood of understanding the intent and meaning of the message. But in Indian schools English grammar teaching-learning has remained a major problem. Moreover, lack of structured integration of grammar in part or a whole is a very common learning barrier of English Language. In Indian schools the teachers need to focus our efforts on strengthening understanding and use of correct English grammar.

3.3.4 Lack of using Teaching-Learning aids

Teaching of English in all its skill domains needs appropriate use of teaching aids and learning materials specifically prepared by language teachers. But in many schools the use of technical devices, audio visual aids, teacher made material is negligibly used even if readily available.

3.3.5 Lack of Practice and Learning Environment

Other than the above constraints, the teachers have very limited teaching hours, mostly from three to six hours per week which are not enough to teach the language. Besides parents do not encourage their children to learn English through speaking with siblings, watching TV programmes, reading English newspapers, etc. Nowadays, children rarely do leisure reading which is very essential to develop language skills.

3.4 Rationale for Implementing RTI English Reading intervention in Indian Schools

Many Indian classrooms may include children who speak several different languages at home. Meeting the needs of diverse readers is a challenging task. In a typical 4th grade classroom, there may be nonreaders, typically developing readers, and students who read at 5th or 6th grade levels or even higher. According to the 10th Annual Status of Education Report (ASER) 2014, Reading levels remain low and unchanged. The report states that only a fourth of all children studying in class 3 can read a class 2 text fluently. Even in class 5 only 50% of the students are able to read class 2 text. Overall, the situation with basic reading continues to be extremely disheartening in India.

3.5 Research Support for RTI English Reading Intervention

The meta - analysis of the National Reading Panel - NRP (2000) found significant benefit of phonemic awareness instruction on children's real - word reading, word decoding, spelling, and reading comprehension. The benefits of phonemic awareness instruction were greatest when instruction focused on just one or two specific phonemic awareness skills, especially phoneme blending and segmentation, as opposed to many phonemic awareness skills, as well as when teachers included phonemic awareness instruction with phonics instruction, particularly in activities involving children's manipulation of letters. Furthermore, studies devoting modest amounts of time to phonemic awareness instruction (e.g.5-18 hours) actually yielded higher effect sizes than those devoting greater amounts of time to phonemic awareness instruction (Ehri, 2004). This finding suggests that relatively small amounts of time devoted to research based phonemic awareness instruction during the appropriate developmental period (pre-K to early Grade 1 for typical students) can yield substantial benefits for children's reading and spelling.

Decades of research (Adams, 1990; Anderson et al., 1985; Chall, 1967; Liberman & Liberman, 1990) established the value of explicit, systematic phonics in teaching young children to read even before. However, more recent studies (e.g., Christensen and Bowey, 2005) suggest particular benefits for a specific type of phonics instruction, synthetic phonics, as opposed to whole-word, analytic phonics approaches. Whole-word approaches emphasize decoding an unknown word by analogy to a known word or inferring phonics relationships through analysis of known, whole words. In these approaches, a child might learn to decode the unfamiliar word bright by comparison to the known word 'might' or by learning word families such as *might, sight, right,* and *tight,* during which the child is expected to infer the pronunciation of '-ight' and apply it to 'bright'. In contrast, synthetic phonics involves parts-to-whole instruction. Children learn sounds for letters and letter patterns as well as how to blend those sounds to form words (e.g., by sounding out /b/,/r/, /i/, /t/ then blending those sounds into bright.)

3.6 Reading Development Profile

Five components of reading

Component	Definition	Examples of assessment tasks
Phonemic awareness	Awareness of, sensitivity to, and ability to manipulate individual phonemes (sounds) in spoken words	Students are asked to blend orally presented phonemes into a spoken word (e.g., "What's this word? /m/ /a/ /sh/") or segment a spoken word into individual phonemes (e.g., "Tell me all the sounds you hear in *mash*.").
Phonics (also called word decoding or word attack)	Knowledge of letter sounds and the ability to apply that knowledge when reading unfamiliar printed words	Students are asked to read unfamiliar words presented out of context (e.g., in a list), with at least some nonsense words (e.g., *strati, gloon*) included.
Fluency	The ability to read grade-appropriate text (passages) accurately, with ease, and with reasonable speed; fluent oral reading also has good intonation and appropriate phrasing (prosody)	Students are asked to read a passage aloud, with the main score of interest the number of words read correctly within a certain time frame, usually 1 minute; a rubric may be used to evaluate prosody.
Vocabulary	Knowledge of the meanings of individual words	Students are asked to point to an appropriate picture from a set of options when the examiner says a word aloud (receptive vocabulary) or to name a pictured object (expressive vocabulary).
Comprehension	The ability to understand language that has been read (reading comprehension) or heard (listening comprehension)	Common formats for assessing broad (overall) comprehension include 1) answering questions about a passage that has been read or listened to; 2) cloze or maze, reading/listening to a passage containing blanks and providing a contextually appropriate word to fit in each blank; and 3) retelling the content of a passage that has been read or heard.

Phonemic awareness involves sensitivity to sounds in spoken words as well as the ability to manipulate those sounds, for example, in oral blending or segmentation tasks. Phonemic awareness, which requires full awareness of every speech sound in a word, is the most advanced level of *phonological awareness,* a broad umbrella term that also encompasses rudimentary levels of awareness. The rhyming words of word *"goat"* are *"boat, coat, float, note, oat, vote" etc.,* For instance, oral rhyming tasks- "What rhymes with *goat?"-represent* a rudimentary level of phonological awareness. In contrast, completing the task- "Tell me all the sounds you hear in the word *boat" -requires* phonemic awareness, full awareness of each sound in the word. Phonological and phonemic awareness are especially important in the earliest stages of learning to read, because they help children grasp the alphabetic principle that printed letters represent speech sounds in spoken words.

Phonics involves knowledge of letter sounds and the ability to apply that knowledge in decoding unfamiliar printed words. Decoding many English words requires attention to letter patterns such as the *igh*in *night* or the *ee*in *free,* so in order to decode many words successfully, children require knowledge about sounds for common letter patterns as well as for individual letters. Children also need to be able to recognize common roots and affixes (prefixes and suffixes) in words, such as the *un-, -ly,* and *-est*in *unwise, unwisely, wisest, gladly, gladdest, unfair,* and *unfairly,* a skill that informs their spelling and vocabulary knowledge as well as their decoding. Phonics skills develop most rapidly in typical readers in the early- to middle-elementary grades, although struggling readers of any age can have phonics-based difficulties.

Perhaps in part because of their common *phon-* root, phonological awareness, phonemic awareness, and phonics are frequently confused in education (Scarborough & Brady, 2002). Phonological and phonemic awareness are abilities involving oral language. Phonics skills involve print. However, phonics knowledge and phonemic awareness interact in critical ways in early reading development. For example, a child who can sound out the letters in the printed word *cap* but cannot blend the sounds /k/, /a/, /p/ together to form the spoken word "cap" will have difficulty reading unfamiliar words (although he or she might be able to memorize specific printed words). Likewise, a child with good phoneme blending skills who does not know sounds for letters such as *c, a,* and *p* will not be able to decode despite his or her capable blending. The former child has a phonemic awareness problem and the latter a phonics problem.

Fluency is the ability to read grade-appropriate text with not only accuracy but also ease, appropriate speed, and prosody in oral reading. Prosody involves reading aloud with appropriate phrasing and intonation, for example, a rising intonation at the end of a question. Lack of fluency often creates a drain on reading comprehension; for instance, dysfluent readers with problems based in decoding may struggle so much to decode individual words that they lose track of meaning. Poor fluency also may reduce motivation to read, as people rarely want to perform for enjoyment tasks that they perceive as laborious and difficult-hence the often-heard comments from poor readers such as, "I'd rather have a root canal/clean the toilet/eat spinach than read." In typical readers, fluency develops most rapidly from late first grade through third grade, but additional fluency development continues into the later grades.

Vocabulary involves knowledge of word meanings and understanding the meaning of words (receptive vocabulary), as well as having the ability to retrieve words and use them appropriately (expressive vocabulary). Vocabulary knowledge is important to success in reading at all grade levels, but it becomes especially important beyond third grade because of increases in the vocabulary demands of the texts used at later grade levels.

Comprehension involves the ability to understand what has been read or heard-not only individual sentences but also longer discourse such as passages and lengthy texts. Discussions of the five components from the NRP report typically include reading comprehension as well as oral language comprehension under the comprehension component, but technically, only oral language comprehension is a component ability because reading comprehension cannot be a component of itself. As with vocabulary, oral comprehension of sentences and longer discourse is important to reading success at all grade levels, but it becomes increasingly critical beyond third grade due to the escalating comprehension demands of texts used at later grade levels.

3.7 RTI for English Reading

The Response to Intervention (RTI) model holds significant promise for better serving English reading for those who are at-risk for academic difficulties. RTI is an instructional model that aims at prevention and early intervention through a tiered system of instructional support—one that adds layers of instructional support to the standard core curriculum delivered in a school, based on the demonstrated and changing needs of the student learners. This includes levels of intervention and instruction that increase in duration and intensity over time; as students improve, measured by reliable and valid assessments, the extra supports are removed.

3.8 Intensity of Tier II and Tier III Intervention

Interventions at Tier 2 involve instructional programs that are aimed at a level of skill development considered to be further along the continuum of skill acquisition than that seen at Tier 3. For example, a 2nd grade student who has been placed into Tier 2 for reading may already have well-developed skills in phonics and alphabetic principles underlying the reading process but may be struggling with the development of fluency in reading connected text. By contrast, a similar 2nd grade student identified as being at high risk and placed into Tier 3 may lack the more foundational skills of decoding and need intensive work on phonics. Thus the Tier II and III Instruction are different based on the nature of the instructional program, which is directly matched to the student's level of identified risk.

The same intervention used for some students at Tier II and III in the RTI intervention programme but the difference is the amount of time spent for instruction of students. For example Letter-sound correspondence, Tier III students may receive many sessions with a particular intervention and Tier II students may spend two or three sessions focused on enhancing the skill development.

3.9 Method adopted for RTI English Reading Intervention

The Indian RTI model adapted the Reading intervention based on US model. The instructional strategies for intervention include: a) differentiated Instruction b) making instruction more explicit: c) providing Systematic Instruction; d) increasing opportunities for practice; and e) monitoring students' Progress and re-teaching when necessary. Each method is detailed below:

3.9.1 Differentiated Instruction

It means teaching same concepts to all students using a variety of instructional strategies. Differentiation means tailoring instruction to meet individual needs. To teach the same concept, the teachers differentiate content, process, products to reach every student in the class. For example, for teaching reading, the intervention teachers used differentiating content which includes the following:
1. Using reading materials at varying readability levels
2. Putting text materials on tape
3. Using spelling or vocabulary lists at readiness levels of students
4. Presenting ideas through both auditory and visual means
5. Meeting with small groups to re-teach an idea for struggling learners, or to extend the thinking or skills of advanced learners.

3.9.2 Phonetic Awareness

A systematic skill sequence has been taught to understand the alphabetic principle to use phonems - Graphme relationship in reading. The following skill areas have been taught to students which were a new paradigm in Indian context.

Trehearne (2000) elaborates on the significance of phonological awareness. Phonological awareness is an understanding of the sound structure of language -that is, that language is made up of words, syllables, rhymes, and sounds (phonemes). Students do not have to know how to name letters or their corresponding sounds to demonstrate phonological awareness; it is first learned through oral language. Phonemic awareness is one component of phonological awareness. Phonemic awareness is an understanding of words at the level of individual sounds - how to segment, blend or manipulate individual sounds in words. Phonics is an understanding of sound and letter relationships in language. Phonological awareness is necessary for effective use of phonics in reading and writing.

Examples of Phonemic Awareness Skills

- **Sound and Word discrimination**: What word doesn't belong with the others: "cat", "mat", "bat", "ran"? **"ran"**
- **Rhyming**: What word rhymes with "cat"? **bat**
- **Syllable splitting**: The onset of "cat" is **/k/**, the rime is **/at/**
- **Blending**: What word is made up of the sounds /k/ /a/ /t/? **"cat"**
- **Phonemic segmentation**: What are the sounds in "cat"? **/k/ /a/ /t/**
- **Phoneme deletion**: What is "cat" without the /k/? **"at"**
- **Phoneme manipulation**: What word would you have if you changed the /t/ in cat to an /n/? **"can"**

3.9.3 Sight Word Recognition

The child needs to be introduced to non phonetic words also along with phonetic words. Sight words lists have both phonetic and non-phonetic words. Sight words introduce the concept of '**Whole Word Method** of Reading'. It means the child has to treat the word as a whole "**Look & Read**". Words are not to be **spelt and read**.

A two year old child who is taken to a supermarket identifies his favourite "5 Star Chocolate", "Milk Bikis" etc. How does it happen? The colour used and letters which appear as colour coded pictures on a definite background help the child to identify the same. This is the first introduction to sight reading. Similarly, when we show letters and words to Pre-kinder and kindergarten children they identify the same. It forms an image in the mind. They visualise the verbals and verbalise the visuals. Thus the sight words initiate Reading.

Sight words in the reading instruction refers to the set of about 100 **words** that keeps reappearing on almost any page of text, "the, he, am, of, their, me" are a few examples. Sight words instruction is an excellent supplement to phonics instruction. Sight word recognition is a key area that was focused in Indian RTI intervention to increase fluency. To introduce a new sight word, the teachers used five teaching techniques

1. See & Say - students see the word on the flash card and say the word while underlining it with his/her finger.
2. Spell Reading - students say the word and spell out the letters, then read the word again.
3. Arm Tapping -students say the word and then spell out the letters while tapping them on his/her arm, then read the word again.
4. Air Writing - students say the word, then writes the letters in the air in front of the flash card.
5. Writing - students write the letters on his/her note book, first looking at and then not looking at the flash card.

Students in Tier3 were also able to recognize sight words when these techniques were used.

3.9.4 Fluency

The fluency instruction gives opportunities for repeated oral reading that includes support and feedback.

- *Guided Reading - reading along with the teacher*

This is the instruction for homogeneously grouped readers. During this time, you carefully provide systematic instruction in the teaching of fluency, word study, and comprehension.

Procedure
- The teacher works with a small group of students with similar needs.
- The teacher provides introductions to the text that support children's later attempts at problem solving.
- Each student reads the whole text or a unified part of the text.
- Readers figure out new words while reading for meaning.
- The teacher prompts, encourages, and confirms students' attempts at problem solving.
- The teacher and student engage in meaningful conversations about what they are reading.
- The teacher and student revisit the text to demonstrate and use a range of comprehension strategies.

- *Repeated Reading - allow the students to re-read the passage*

The teacher models fluent reading of the selected passage, then discusses new vocabulary and content with the students. The group practices the text as a whole group. Students practice the passage independently until they have reached the desired criterion or have read the passages a specified number of times.

The studies on Repeated Reading have found clear improvements across multiple readings regardless of students' reading levels or age levels, although greater gains were sometimes attributed to poor readers (National Reading Panel, pp. 3-15). Repeated Reading can be incorporated into a regular classroom reading program. This technique can be modified to include unassisted or assisted repeated-reading techniques. The investigations on repeated reading suggest that fluency can be improved through repeated readings with or without specific guidance; students can work independently or with support from an adult or peer. Text selections need to be based on students' reading levels. The teacher needs to set the context for rereading so that students don't think of it as a punitive or remedial technique.

- *Partner Reading - In partner reading, paired students take turns reading aloud to each other*

In partner reading, students take turns reading aloud to each other. Students are divided into pairs. Each student reads a short passage three times and then provides feedback about their own and their partner's oral fluent reading behaviors. For partner reading, partners can have the same reading ability or partnerships can include a more fluent reader with a less fluent reader. Many types of reading materials can be used, such as passages from basal readers, student produced stories, and trade books

Partner reading enables teachers to use repeated reading with a minimum of management difficulties. This strategy gives beginning readers or older students with reading difficulties and opportunity to read contextual materials a number of times so they can experience fluent reading. A typical paired, repeated reading activity takes about 10 to 15 minutes. Many types of reading material can be used, such as passages from basal readers, student-produced stories, or trade books.

3.9.5 *Comprehension*

Strategies have been used to the reach comprehension once they attain minimal level of fluency. The strategies include:

- repeated reading with comprehension practice
- story map to increase comprehension
  - o Teacher introduces simple story concepts (e.g., characters, setting, plot and/or problems to be solved).
  - o Teacher gives each student a blank story map.
  - o Students look for story concepts/elements and write them in the blank spaces on the map.
  - o Students discuss their responses with the teacher

3.10 Preparation of Lesson Plan and Materials for Intervention

A lesson plan is a detailed guide for teaching a lesson. It's a step-by-step guide that outlines the teacher's objectives for what the students will accomplish that day. Creating a lesson plan involves setting goals, developing activities, and determining the materials that will be used.

Lesson plan helps teachers to stay on track and it also helps them to prepare for every step of the lesson. It also helps the teacher to achieve their objectives on students' achievement.

In the research project, lesson plan has been prepared for eight components for English reading

- i)   Singing alphabet song
- ii)   Blending Two to Five Phoneme words
- iii)   Guided Reading
- iv)   Incremental Rehearsal
- v)   Phonetic awareness - Identifying words

vi) Sight words

vii) Letter shape and letter Name correspondence - Letter Naming Fluency

viii) Partner Reading

ix) Building Fluency and Comprehension

3.11 Teaching English Reading

3.11.1 Lesson Plan 1

Teaching Component: Sight Word Recognition

Focus:

Building sight word vocabulary by modeling and guided practice. Sight word means frequently used words. Selected sight words *I, a, can, we, run and play*. Selected words should include familiar and new words.

Materials Needed

1. **Sight word cards (single cards)**

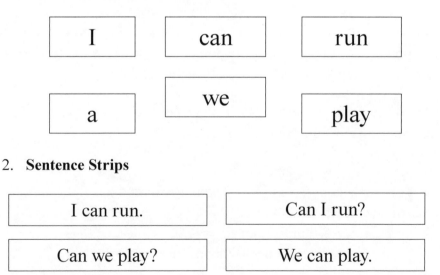

2. **Sentence Strips**

| I can run. | Can I run? |
| Can we play? | We can play. |

Direction

Step 1: Provide students with instruction on how the lesson format will run. Give students a purpose for learning sight words.

Step 2: Teacher shows the word card and says the word aloud

Step 3: Student sees the targeted word and listens to the teacher say the word and then student says the word aloud

Step 4: Teacher introduces the next word and repeats the above procedure for each new word

Step 5: Review the sight words randomly. If the student says the word correctly say 'good', when the student responds with the incorrect response, it should be corrected immediately. That word should be shown again within the next 2 words to check for recall.

Step 6: All sentences are displayed. Teacher reads through all sentences with students chorally. Teacher models reading the sentence (I Do). Students keep moving the finger on the strip and listen to the teacher

Step 7: Give the sentence strips to each student

Step 8: Students read aloud the sentence along with the teacher (We Do)

Step 9: Students read the sentence without prompting by the teacher (You Do)

Step 10: Continue procedure for all sentence strips

Step 11: Review the students randomly with targeted sight word strips, the incorrect response to be corrected immediately.

Step 12: The next class starts with reviewing learnt words and new-targeted words to be introduced.

Step 13: Periodically review the words of all lessons.

3.11.2 Lesson Plan 2

Lesson title: Blending Two to Five Phoneme Words -Lesson 1 (30 minutes)

Lesson goal: Blending two or fivephoneme wordsusing sound spelling through direct instruction, which helps to increase oral reading fluency.

Lesson objectives:
1. The students will understand and soundout individual sounds in the presented words with 90% accuracy.
2. The students will be able to blend the sounds to read the presented words with 90% accuracy.

Materials& Instructor Preparation:
1. Sound revision chart with targeted list of sounds
2. Two to five phoneme wordcards depending on grade level and Tier (the word cards should include a representation of V (vowel) C (consonant), CVC, VCC, CVCC, CCVC, CCVCC, CCCVC, and CCCVCC words and their combinations tailored to the grade level and Tier
3. Printed copies of two to five phoneme word sheets for individual students

Types of reinforcement:
Verbal: Excellent, you did well
Non-verbal: Stars to be stuck by the student name if he/she did well on that day
Blending game using a tablet for a selected student(s) during the last 5 minutes of the lesson

Student response types (in order you will use them)
I
My Turn (Teacher modeling)
We Do (Teacher and students together doing the task)
You do (Students repeat the same procedure)
II
Teacher waves hand: choral response
Teacher points to two students: paired response
Teacher points to one student: individual response

Advance organizer (preparing students for lesson)

Motivating students: Rationale for learning the skill *(We are going to learn and practice blending of sounds into words, which will help you to become good readers)*

Posing questions to students

1. Do all letters have sounds?
2. Provide examples of some of the sounds letters make, including both consonants and vowels

Explaining about (with sample words and posing questions)

1. What is a word?
2. How do words look?
3. Say and write some words and point out the different sounds
4. Explain that all sentences we speak/write are made up of words
5. Explain how we read a word in English by blending sounds.
6. Explain about blending as adding sounds and pushing together to read a word: model with an example word 'man'.

Step-by-step instruction

I. Pre-teaching

1. Model the targeted letter sounds with the letter sounds chart with all the students
2. Distinguish between sounds for consonants and vowels
3. Show two to five phoneme words and model how to break the sounds and find how many sounds there are in the word? (by taping with index finger on the table for each sound)
4. Break down the sounds and count how many sounds there are in a particular word (by tapping with index finger on the table for each sound)

II. Main Lesson Instruction

1. I Do: Teacher explains the task for the first word
   • Show the word card and say each letter sound in the word
   • Tap the corresponding letter as you say each sound

- Swipe the finger slowly from left to right and blend the sounds slowly
- In 4-5 phoneme words, first blend sounds into syllables and subsequently into words
- Blend the sounds faster to read the whole word
2. Explain the task for the same word again for better understanding
3. We do: Teacher and students together do the task for the same word
4. You Do: Students practice blending for the word in choral.
5. Ensure that the students understand how to say individual sounds and to blend the sounds together to read a word.
6. If students make a mistake, model the step correctly and have the students repeat it until providing a correct response
7. Repeat the guided practice for all the listed words. Start with from easy to more difficult.

Word game
1. Say the whole word ask the students to say the sounds in the word
2. Say the sounds in a word and ask the students to put the sounds in their mind together and say the word when called on

Lesson Review
Tell students that today they have learned to sound out words and to blend the sounds to read each word
Tell the students that they started from easy words and also learned some harder ones
Tell the students that reading in English is blending sounds together to read each word

Lesson Mastery Assessment
1. Say sounds in a word and ask students to say the word (Choral/ pair/individual)
2. Show a word card and ask the students to blend the sounds and say the word (Choral/pair/individual)

3.11.3 Lesson Plan 3

Lesson Title: Building Fluency with Partner Reading

Lesson Goal
Increase students' accuracy and fluency in reading connected text to practice reading a passage and working with a partner to achieve determined fluency goals.

Lesson Objectives
1. Students read the passage with 90% accuracy.
2. Students demonstrate abilty to achieve fluency goal determined by the teacher.

Materials & Instructor Preparation
1. Individual Copies of Instructional-level pre-counted passages selected based on students' reading levels (see attached sample).
2. Copies of Individual student graphs.
3. Stop Watch

Reinforcement
1. In this lesson reinforcement should be given to the pairs for following the partner reading steps.
2. Inform the students to reinforce their partner verbally after completion of reading the passage.

Verbal: Super
1. The teacher will provide with stars stick under student graphs based on their level of reaching the fluency goal.

Students Response Types (in order you will use them)
1. In this lesson, students will be asked to respond by reading the passage
   - Initiate the lesson using preview reading and ask for unfamiliar words

- As students practice reading with partner.
- As students begin to demonstrate accuracy move to individual reading when it is clear that students are able to correctly

Advance Organizer (preparing students for lesson)
1. Inform the students that rationale of the lesson
   "Today we are going to read passage with the help of your friends Remember, passage is made up of sentences that tell us about people, places and things."
2. Discuss about the structure of a passage
3. Explain about working with partner for achieving reading goal.

Step-by-step Instruction

I. Pre Teaching

Fluent reading
1. Introduce the student fluent reading with word list they can read accurately.
2. Have the word list chart.
3. Model fluent reading -Inform students *"When we read words in sentences, we must read the words quickly. Listen as I read the words quickly"*
4. Place the copies of word list before each student(Randomly change the order of words on the list for each student)
5. Ask the student to read the word list individually as quick as they can.
6. Prompt students to read the words quickly.
7. If any student produces an incorrect response, repeat the teacher model instruction.

Previewing the passage
1. Hand out the copies of selected instructional level passage to students.
2. Model reading the selected instructional level passage to the students.

3. Ask the students to follow as you read with their fingers.
4. Ask the students to preview the passage silently on their own and identify any words they do not know.
   "I want you to read the sentences silently and raise your hand if you come to a word you don't know"
5. Have the students preview the passage and if they do not know any word provide the correct word for the students.

II. Main lesson Instruction

1. Explain to students that they will be working with a partner to increase their accuracy and fluency when reading passage.
   "Today you will be working with a partner to practice reading a short passage."
2. Pair the students according to their reading level - Partners consist of a higher performing reader working with a lower performing reader.
   "Practicing reading short passages will help you to learn to read faster and remember what you have read."
3. Introduce the fluency goal for the lesson
   "Your goal for today is to correctly read 30 words in one minute."
   Discuss with students about fluency goal - the expected number of words they can read correctly in a minute.
4. Explicitly introduce the procedure to the students.
   Model the partner reading procedure with a student and have the students observe and ask for doubts.
   "Observe the procedure as I do with my partner."
   a. Select a student (low performing student) as your partner and have his/her sit near to you.
   b. Have the copies of selected passage with your partner.
   c. Say the student that you are partner1 and he/she is partner2 and explains partner1 reads first and the other reads next to you.
   d. Provide model reading for the student
   e. Ask the student (partner 2) to read the passage

f. Provide correct word for the student (partner 2) of he/she did mistake.

g. Ask the student (partner 2) to practice reading for three times along with you.

h. After completion of all these instruct the students to initiate for individual reading.

i. Model individual reading with the student (partner 2)

j. Have he/she time one minute for your reading ("first timing.")

k. Have other higher performing student to mark incorrect words you read and count and tell the correct words you read. - Explain the students that you will do this for them while they are doing individual reading.

l. Have the student (partner 2) to mark (shade) up to the number of word you read correctly in your graph.

5. Instruct the students if the two partners don't know any word ask the students to have the teachers help.

6. Hand out the copies of passage and graph to individual students

7. Pair the students according to their reading level (higher performing reader with lower performing reader) and tell who is partner1 and wo is partner2.

8. Ask the partner1 (higher performing reader) to model reading to his/her pair.

9. Monitor the student pairs for reading accuracy and give feedback and correct words as per pairs need.

10. After that ask the partner 2 (lower performing student) to read the passage for three times along with the partner 1 and teacher should monitor and provide help if they needed.

11. Instruct to raise the hand once they are ready for individual reading.

12. Have the student read individually as quickly and the other partner time for one minute.

13. The teacher note the correct words read by the student and have the partner to record in graph by shading up to the correct number of words.

14. While students practice reading the passage, the teacher observes to make sure that students are modeling the passage reading,

providing appropriate feedback, reading the passages the required number of times, and graphing their progress.

15. Discuss with students on have they achieved their fluency goal? (30 word per minute)
16. Provide feedback and suggestions to improve fluency.

Lesson Review:

1. Review what you did during the lesson today focusing on the following:
   a. We learnt to read passage as fluently as you can
   b. We read the passage to achieve our fluency goal
   c. Have any student to model fluent reading with partner
   d. Have any student model fluent reading individually
   e. Have any student model timing for one minute ad graphing correct word read by the partner

Lesson mastery Assessment:

1. Read the Passage accurately in pair
2. Read the passage fluently as much the student can

Sample lesson
The Dog and the Log

It was a warm summer day. The sun was hot on the	12
dog. So the dog went to the lake for a swim. The dog	25
went to the side of the lake. He looked at the lake. He	38
saw a big log on the lake. He said, "I will get that log."	52
The dog swam to the log. The log was big. The dog	64
said, "That log is too big. I can not get the log. I will get	79
on the log." So the dog got on the log.	89

References

- Adams, M. (1990). Beginning to read: Thinking and learning about print. Cambridge, MA: MIT Press.
- Alexander, R. (2000). Culture and pedagogy: International comparisons in primary education. Oxford, UK: Blackwell.
- Anderson, R. A., Heibert, E. H., Scott, J. A., & Wilkinson, I. A. G. with contributions from members of the Commission on Reading (1985). Becoming a nation of readers: The report of the Commission on Reading. Washington, D.C. The National Institute of Education.
- Chall, J.S. (1967). Learning to read: The great debate. New York: McGraw-Hill.
- Christensen, C.A and Bowey, J.A (2005). The efficacy of orthographic rime, grapheme-phoneme correspondence, and implicit phonics approaches to teaching decoding skills. Scientific Studies of Reading.; 9:327-349.
- Clarke, P. (2001). Teaching and learning: the culture of pedagogy. New Delhi, India: Sage Publications.
- Clay, M. (1991). Becoming literate: The construction of inner control. Portsmouth, NH: Heinemann Education.
- Ehri, C (2004), Development of Sight Word Reading: Phases and Findings P.135-154
- Frater, G and Staniland, A (1994). Reading Recovery in New Zealand: A report from the Office of Her Majesty's Chief Inspector of Schools. Literacy, Teaching and Learning: An International Journal of Early Literacy, 1(1), 143-162.
- Holdaway, E.A (1978). Facet and overall satisfaction of teachers. Educational Administration Quarterly, 14(1), 30-47.
- Liberman, I.Y and & Liberman, A.M (1990). Whole word vs. code emphasis: Underlying assumptions and their implications for reading instruction. Bulletin of the Orton Society, 40, 51-76.

- OSR Journal of Humanities And Social Science (IOSR-JHSS), 19(1), Ver. IX (Feb. 2014), PP 101-116 e-ISSN: 2279-0837, p-ISSN: 2279-0845.
- Scarborough, H., & Brady, S (2002). Toward a common terminology for talking about speech and reading: A glossary of the "phon" words and some related terms. Journal of Literacy Research, 34, 299-336.
- Spear-Swerling, L., & Sternberg, R.J. [1996]. *Off track: When poor readers become "learning disabled."* Boulder, CO: Westview Press.

4

Mathematics Instruction in RTI: Indian Context

R.Nagomi Ruth, M.Revathi and T.Gomathi

One of the core academic subjects throughout the world is mathematics. Mathematics comprises many important skills required in typical daily activities (e.g., shopping, banking, cooking, and household activities). Further, in today's increasingly technological and technologically dependent society, more and more jobs are related to mathematics and science. Because of this, it is critical that students begin to develop essential mathematic concepts and skills beginning at an early age. However, studies conducted over two decades have shown that students in many countries including in the United States do not perform well on mathematics.

4.1 Research Findings

Studies such as those below have raised concerns about the adequacy of mathematics instruction:

- In a 1988 study of the mathematics proficiency of thirteen-year-old students from six countries, students from the United States had the lowest scores. (Lapointe, Meade, & Phillips, 1989)
- In 1999, the Trends in International Mathematics and Science Study (TIMSS) indicated that eighth-grade students in the United States were outperformed by students in eighteen countries in mathematics proficiency. (Mullis, Martin, Gonzalez, Gregory, Garden, O'Connor, Chrostowski, & Smith, 2000)

In India a growing proportion of Grade II children did not know numbers 1 to 9. This means that they are were learning them in Grade I. Increasing numbers of children in Grade III did not recognize numbers till 100. This means that they did not pick them up in Grade II. Half of all children in Grade V have not yet learned basic skills that they should have learned by Grade II. Hence strong focus is needed in Grade I & II to ensure that basic skills are built in these early years. **(Annual Status of Education Report 2014, by PRATHAM: study conducted in 577 rural districts in India)**

In primary schools the Indian curriculum, mathematical facts often are taught through rote learning. This method is expected to build a strong base for the formation of higher concepts effectively. Developing rapid mental calculation skills is emphasized from an early age. From eighth grade, students follow a course structure that includes number, algebra, geometry, and statistics. Although eighth grade courses include examples to give students an opportunity to practice mathematical knowledge and skills in context, the curriculum is being developed to promote more problem solving in real life contexts. (Central Board of Secondary Education. (2012). *Overview*. Retrieved from http://cbse.nic.in/ & Council for the Indian School Certificate Examinations. (2011).

In Indian context the focus of instruction is usually on teaching computational procedures and allowing students time for repeated practice, rather than exploring a given mathematic concept and how it connects to other mathematic concepts. In addition, evidence based practices are not used extensively.

Key findings in the literature highlight the need to focus on early mathematics instruction:

1. Children who have had less experience or exposure to mathematical concepts and numeracy are at high risk for mathematics failure (Griffin & Case, 1997).

2. Most students fail to meet minimal mathematics proficiency standards by the end of their formal schooling (U.S. Department of Education, 2003).

3. Students identified with specific learning disabilities perform lower and grow at a slower pace relative to their peers in learning mathematics.

4. Existing instructional tools and textbooks often do a poor job of adhering to important instructional principles for learning in mathematics (National Mathematics Advisory Panel, 2008).

5. Math is highly proceduralized and continually builds on previous knowledge for successful learning. Hence, early deficits have enduring and devastating effects on later learning, as indicated in *The Head Start Path to Positive Child Outcomes* (U.S. Department of Health and Human Services, 2001) and elsewhere (e.g., National Mathematics Advisory Panel, 2008; National Council of Teachers of Mathematics [NCTM], 2000; U.S. Department of Education, 2003).

6. Early mathematics intervention can repair deficits and prevent future deficits (Clements & Sarama, 2007; Fuchs, Fuchs, & Karns, 2001; Fuchs, Fuchs, Yazdian, & Powell, 2002; Griffin & Case, 1997; Sophian, 2004).

Response to Intervention (RTI) has become a vehicle for system reform because it provides a framework in which data can be relied on as the basis for making relative judgments as determining who needs help the most and how much they need and for distributing instructional resources to promote the greatest good for the greatest number of students. In Indian context, Response to Intervention model was piloted and the outcomes revealed that RTI model is effective to enhance learning of mathematics subject.

CBM measures prepared for Indian primary school children have been found to yield reliable scores. Intervention procedures have been adapted from the research partners from the University of Minnesota, USA and the materials have been prepared suiting to the need of students in India. In order to change math learning outcomes, the quality of instruction needs to be changed. Burns, VanDerHeyden, & Boice (2008) stated explicit /direct instruction is effective to teach mathematics. In the RTI intervention process. Explicit instruction is adopted to teach students in all the 3 tiers.

Explicit instruction is systematic, direct, engaging, and success oriented-and has been shown to promote achievement for all students. This highly practical and accessible resource gives special and general education teachers the tools to implement explicit instruction in any grade level or content area. If a teacher want to change math learning outcomes, he/she was to change the quality of the instructional interaction between student and teacher. So what are the characteristics of quality core instruction in mathematics?

Explicit or direct instruction involves teaching a specific skill or concept in a highly structured environment using clear, direct language. This type of instruction is focused on producing specific learning outcomes and sometimes involves the use of scripted lessons. During explicit instruction, the teacher clearly identifies the expectations for learning, highlights important details of the concept or skill, provides precise instructions, and connects new learning to previously learned material. There is the explanation of this instructional strategy.

4.2 Steps in an Explicit or Direct Instruction Lesson

4.2.1 Orientation to the Lesson

- Teacher gains students' attention
- Teacher relates today's lesson to a previously related one
- Teacher uses essential questions to activate students' thinking

4.2.2   Initial Instruction

- Teacher leads completion of several sample problems
- Teacher models and instructs students to model problem completion
- Teacher points out difficult aspects of problem

4.2.3   Teacher-Guided Practice

- Students complete problems under teacher supervision
- Teacher monitors each student's success in problem completion
- Teacher assists students independently
- Students may discuss problems with each other

4.2.4   Independent Practice

- Students complete sample problems independently
- Students may complete homework as independent practice

4.2.5   Check

- Teacher checks student performance on independent work

4.2.6   Reteach

Teacher identifies students with continuing difficulty and reteaches the skills

Like most instructional methods, the Direct Instruction Model is a blend of getting students ready to learn, teaching, guiding them in practice, then allowing them to practice independently. The method comes from the educational theory that people learn best with direct, explicit, and focused instruction followed by a gradual release of responsibility. Traditional models are more strict without class conversations and activities. A sample lesson plan is given here.

4.3 Lesson Plan

Grade: I
Title: Currency (Rupees)
Time allotted: 45 minutes

Overview

This lesson will enable students to know that money is used in their everyday lives. The students will learn about money, why we have it, what we do with it, and what it is worth. This lesson has been designed to assess prior knowledge of the students and will show them the basic skills they need in order to use money correctly. They will become comfortable using money in their everyday lives. The strategy being used is behavioral model teaching.

Goals:

The student will understand the concept of money and will use it in their every day lives. The student will understand and demonstrate how to count money and will apply these skills to their every day environment.

Objectives:

Given a group of manipulative (e.g. Different coins, Rupee notes of 10, 20, 50, 100, 500, 2000) and the directions, "what is this," the student will tell the teacher the correct name of the coin and the currency note(rupee). The teacher holds it in his/her hand and prompts the students for 5 consecutive trails to name the currency.

Materials:

Coins for Rupee: 1, 2, 5, and 10
Rupee notes for: 5, 10, 20, 50, 100, 500 and 2000
The money allotted will be plastic money used for play.

83

Anticipatory Set:

At the beginning of the lesson I will get the students' attention by saying good morning/ good afternoon and get their attention. I will then proceed by holding up the currency notes in my hand and asking the students *"what it is,"* *"where have you seen this before,"* and *"what do you do with it?"* The student will shout out a number of ideas and I will answer them yes or no depending on what their answer is.

This will take 4- 5 minutes. At the end of this process I will tell the students that the lesson is on money and that it is important to know what money is and how to use it because you will apply this skill to your every day life.

Direct Teaching

Depending on the student's prior knowledge, I will then start by explaining what money is. Once they have gained mastery of this, I will explain why we use money. I will inform them that with out money there would be chaos, everything would be free and no one would be able to keep track of their belongings. Next, I will explain to the students that we buy things with money and that money is used in our everyday lives. I will ask the students if they can give me some ideas of where we use money and then I will bring them up to date by explaining that we use money when we buy food, clothes, fill our cars up with gas, travel, and purchase things. Finally, I will notify that students that we see money all over and I will explain that different places have different looking money. (Depending on your students, you may want to bring in different kinds of money to show the students)

Guided Practice

Now, let's do it together!

The teacher will have a list of amounts that she wants the student to make using their allotted money. (The students are to use the least amount of money possible to get the answer/simplest form.) The teacher will walk around the room and guide the student if necessary. The student will complete this task and then the teacher will move on to the next idea of the lesson.

Closure

For the closure, I will ask the students to write, on a piece of paper, three things they learned from the lesson. They will hand it in and I will call on a student to tell me one thing they learned that way they get comfortable speaking in front of the class and it will also help to refresh the other student's minds. I will choose these names by pulling Popsicle sticks from a cup. Each stick with have a students name on it, once that student has been chosen I will put it off to the side that way each child will have a chance to share their idea.

Independent Practice:

Now, try it on your own!

A worksheet will be handed out to the students. The work sheet will have pictures of money on it and the student will have to write the correct amount showed on the worksheet. If time precedes, the student can work on this quietly at their desk, if there is no time, the student will complete the given task at home for homework and the teacher will collect it the following day.

The teacher may also assign a page in the students' text book for them to complete at home or quietly at their desk. This too will be collected.

Attached is another sheet that the students could do for homework or if they finish everything before the other students. It's called money, money, money. The student has to count the change and write the total number given.

Accommodations

Each of the students will all be allotted enough time for each question. I will be walking around the class room to help the child who may need it. As for ESL students, I will be able to repeat the number to them in their language. If they don't work, then I will have a written amount in their language to help them better understand the numbers.

Evaluation/Assessment

To assess the students I will give them a test. It will test the students in two ways. The first part of the test will be a picture of an allotted amount and they will have to write the amount shown. For the second part of the test, I will provide the students with an amount and they will have to write out (in smallest form) what they would use to show that amount.

Mathematics interventions at the Tier 2 (secondary prevention) level of a multi-tier prevention system must incorporate six instructional principles:

1. Instructional explicitness
2. Instructional design that eases the learning challenge
3. A strong conceptual basis for procedures that are taught
4. An emphasis on drill and practice
5. Cumulative review as part of drill and practice
6. Motivators to help students regulate their attention and behavior and to work hard

The first principle of effective intervention in mathematics at the secondary prevention level is *instructional explicitness.* Typically developing students profit from the general education mathematics program even though it relies, at least in part, on a constructivist, inductive instructional style. Students who are at risk for serious mathematics deficits, however, fail to profit from those programs in a way that produces understanding of the structure, meaning, and operational requirements of mathematics. A meta-analysis of 58 math studies (Kroesbergen & Van Luit, 2003) revealed that students with math disability benefit more from explicit instruction than from discovery-oriented methods. Therefore, effective intervention in Tier 2 requires an explicit, didactic form of instruction in which the teacher directly shares the information the child needs to learn.

4.4 Peer Tutoring

Peer tutoring method is useful for intervention. In which two students work together on an instructional activity. For learning multiplication tables in Grade I, peer tutoring is effective.

In *peer tutoring*, two students work together on an instructional activity (e.g., learning multiplication tables, practicing two-digit addition with carrying). The pairs of students can be of the same or different ability levels. Two peer-tutoring approaches (i.e., Peer Assisted Learning Strategies [PALS] Math, Class Wide Peer Tutoring for mathematics) have been shown through research to be highly effective for teaching mathematics. These strategies have several features in common.

Class-wide peer tutoring is found to be effective in improving students' grades, increasing knowledge of subject matter, developing students' engagement and improving students' behavior in the class room. Peer tutoring to improve achievement level of students in the math, reading, vocabulary, social studies and English.

Peer tutoring is used for intervention of Tier1 and Tier2 intervention. In peer tutoring, two students work together on an instructional activity (e.g two digit addition with carrying). Students in Tier1 and Tier students have been engaged in peer tutoring during the research period.

4.5 Intervention using Peer tutoring

This intervention employs students as reciprocal peer tutors to target acquisition of basic math computation using constant time delay (Menesses & Gresham, 2009; Telecsan, Slaton, & Stevens, 1999). Each tutoring 'session' is brief and includes its own progress-monitoring component making this a convenient and time-efficient math intervention.

4.5.1 Intervention Steps

Students participating in the tutoring program meet in a setting in which their tutoring activities will not distract other students. The setting is supervised by an adult who monitors the students and times the tutoring activities. These are the steps of the tutoring intervention:

4.5.2 Complete the Tutoring Activity

In each tutoring pair, one of the students assumes the role of tutor. The teacher (timer) starts the timer and says 'Begin' and after 3 minutes, the timer and says 'Stop'.

While the timer is running, the tutor follows this sequence. Tutor teaches the preliminary idea of the concept for 3minutes. When the tutee responds correctly, the tutor acknowledges the correct answer and proceeds to the next step. When the tutee does not respond or respond incorrectly, the tutor states the correct answer and has the tutee repeat the correct answer.

Switch Roles. After the tutor has completed the 3-minute tutoring activity and assessed the tutee's progress on math facts, the two students reverse roles. The new tutor then implements steps 2 and 3 described above with the new tutee.

4.5.3 *Monitor Student Performance*

As the student pairs complete the tutoring activities, the teacher monitors the integrity with which the intervention is carried out. At the conclusion of the tutoring session, the adult gives feedback to the student pairs, praising successful implementation and providing corrective feedback to students as needed. Teachers can use the form *Peer Tutoring in Math Computation with Constant Time Delay: Integrity Checklist* (see bottom of page) to conduct integrity checks of the intervention and student progress-monitoring components of the math peer tutoring.

The adult supervisor also monitors student progress. After each student pair has completed one tutoring cycle and assessed and recorded their progress, the supervisor reviews the score sheets. If a student has successfully answered all 10 math fact cards three times in succession, the supervisor provides that student's tutor with a new set of math flashcards.

4.6 Error Analysis

Another method of assessing student understanding, or misunderstanding, is to identify and analyze the errors a student repeatedly makes when solving a mathematical problem. If the reasons for the student's incorrect answers are not apparent, the teacher can ask the student to describe the procedure he or she used to solve the problem. In either case, the teacher can use the information from the error analysis to provide instruction to help the student understand the correct procedure for solving the problem. In the example below, the teacher was unable to easily recognize the procedure used by the student to complete the problem, so the teacher asked the student to explain how he solved the problem.

Example: Error Analysis

Student Solutions:

6 8	7 5	5 9
+ 3 5	+ 3 9	+ 6 1
13 9	1410	1011

When explanation was asked, the student answered:

For the first problem, I added 8 + 5 and got 13, so I wrote 13 down. Then I added 6 + 3 and got 9. I wrote the 9 after the 13. So I got 139. I did the same thing for the other problems.

After knowing the idea, the teacher will correct student's mistake

References

1. Burns, M.K., VanDerHeyden, A.M and Boice, C.H (2008). *Best practices in delivery intensive academic interventions.* In A. Thomas & J. Grimes (Eds.) Best practices in school psychology (5th ed.). Bethesda, MD: National Association of School Psychologists.

2. Clements, D.H and Sarama, J (2007). Effects of a Preschool Mathematics Curriculum: Summative Research on the Building Blocks Project, University of Buffalo, State University of New York, Journal for Research in Mathematics Education, 38(2), 136-163.

3. Fuchs, L.S., Fuchs, D., & Karns, K. (2001). Enhancing kindergarteners' mathematical development: Effects of peer-assisted learning strategies. The Elementary School Journal, 101, 495-511.

4. Fuchs, L.S., Fuchs, D., Yazdian, L and Powell, S.R. (2002). Enhancing first-grade children's mathematical development with peer-assisted learning strategies. School Psychology Review, 31, 569-583.

5. Griffin, S., & Case, R. (1997). Rethinking the primary school math curriculum: An approach based on cognitive science. Issues in Education, 3(1), 1-49.

6. LaPointe, A.E., Mead, N.A and Phillips, G. W (1989). A world of differences. Princeton, NJ: Educational Testing Service.

7. Mullis, I.V.S., Martin, M.O., Gonzalez, E.J., Gregory, K.D., Garden, R.A., O'Connor, K.M., Chrostowski, S.J and Smith, T.A. (2000). TIMSS 1999 international mathematics report. Chestnut Hill, MA: Boston College.

8. Sophian, C (2004). Mathematics for the future: Developing a Head Start curriculum to support mathematics learning. *Early Childhood Research Quarterly, 19,* 59-81.

5

RTI in Indian Context: Evidence Based Research

Premavathy Vijayan, G.Victoria Naomi, R.Shanthi, R.Nagomi Ruth and M.Revathi

Response to Intervention (RTI) is a new paradigm in Indian context. RTI is a current topic about which teachers are seeking research information. RTI is the practice of providing quality instruction and intervention and using student learning in response to that instruction to make instructional and important educational decisions (Batsche et al., 2005). After this new model implemented in India and widely popularized the concepts through workshops and seminars during the 3 year research period, it is perhaps the most discussed educational initiative particularly in the Coimbatore schools which are in the southern part of India. It is a school wide program implemented in two model schools for two years (2015 & 2016). Apart from two experimental schools, four control schools have been involved in order to find out the effect of RTI in Indian schools. In this section, the outcomes of the research are discussed.

5.1 Result: 1 Grouping Students in to Tiered Instruction

Based on the universal screening scores, students were grouped for intervention. The first phase of universal screening indicated that a majority (85%) of students was below 50th percentile and hence all students were placed under Tier II intervention for a period of 3 months. After a 3 month intervention, the next universal screening was administered, and based on scores students were regrouped for Tiered instructions. The following table presents the details.

Distribution of Students in Experimental Schools by Tier, Grade and Subject Area

Grade	Subject	Tiered Instruction		
		Tier 1	*Tier 2*	*Tier 3*
	English	55%	27%	18%
3	Tamil	65%	17%	18%
	Math	58%	24%	18%
	English	51%	28%	21%
4	Tamil	65%	15%	19%
	Math	61%	23%	17%
	English	56%	26%	17%
5	Tamil	68%	16%	16%
	Math	64%	19%	17%

5.2 Result 2: English Reading Ability (Grade III to V)

English reading ability of Grade III to V were assessed using oral reading fluency passage and comparison made between experimental and control groups using CBM passages prepared. The V phases of data collection indicate a class of students for example III Grade students participated Phase I to Phase III in the same Grade and IV & V phases of tests were administered when they moved to upper Grade (IV Grade). In the research it is considered as V phases of data for a single grade. Data from all five phases and included here.

Data Collection Phase	Condition	Mean	Std. Deviation	N
Phase I	Experimental	2.9250	2.83194	40
	Control	2.7055	2.99749	73
	Total	2.7832	2.92913	113
Phase II	Experimental	6.8125	6.03695	40
	Control	5.7877	6.30527	73
	Total	6.1504	6.20408	113
Phase III	Experimental	5.4750	6.41308	40
	Control	4.4452	4.88092	73
	Total	4.8097	5.46634	113
Phase IV	Experimental	18.0500	12.64394	40
	Control	7.1027	9.84426	73
	Total	10.9779	12.06722	113
Phase V	Experimental	27.2750	14.00227	40
	Control	10.5890	14.22985	73
	Total	16.4956	16.20743	113

The above data represent mean scores and standard deviations of students in both the experimental and control groups on CBM English reading aloud measures. The scores are the number of words read correctly in 1 minute. Below is the graphical representation of the mean scores across the five phases of data collection.

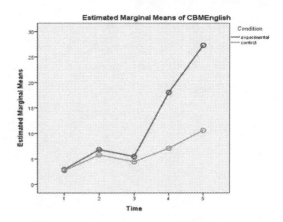

Figure 1: CBM English reading - Grade 3

The blue line represent the number of words read correctly in the two model schools, while the green line represents the same metric for students in the for control schools.

5.3 Result 3: English Reading Ability (Grade IV)

English reading ability of Grade IV was assessed using oral reading fluency passage and comparison made between experimental and control groups.

Data Collection Phase	Condition	Mean	Std. Deviation	N
Phase I	Experimental	6.6957	10.70810	69
	Control	5.0056	6.09932	89
	Total	5.7437	8.43932	158
Phase II	Experimental	11.1594	13.98147	69
	Control	8.2865	9.56286	89
	Total	9.5411	11.74598	158
Phase III	Experimental	11.5870	11.16749	69
	Control	9.8258	9.48387	89
	Total	10.5949	10.25660	158
Phase IV	Experimental	27.5870	21.39835	69
	Control	13.6011	13.15946	89
	Total	19.7089	18.54210	158
Phase V	Experimental	34.9855	21.43063	69
	Control	14.2697	11.88870	89
	Total	23.3165	19.60570	158

The above data represent mean scores and standard deviations of students in both the experimental and control groups on CBM English reading aloud measures. The scores are the number words read correctly in 1 minute. Data from all five phases are included here. Below is the graphical representation of the mean scores across the five phases of data collection.

The blue line represents the number of words read correctly in the two model schools, while the green line represents the same metric for students in the four control schools.

English reading ability of Grade V was assessed using oral reading fluency passage and comparison made between experimental and control groups.

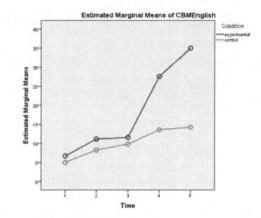

Figure 2. CBM English reading - Grade 4

5.4   Result 4: English Reading Ability (Grade V)

Data Collection Phase	Condition	Mean	Std. Deviation	N
Phase I	Experimental	10.4625	12.39150	80
	Control	12.5125	10.06084	120
	Total	11.6925	11.06794	200
Phase II	Experimental	23.0188	21.80472	80
	Control	18.6583	15.64308	120
	Total	20.4025	18.42994	200
Phase III	Experimental	13.7938	14.11452	80
	Control	14.3000	12.24975	120
	Total	14.0975	12.99543	200
Phase IV	Experimental	31.2375	22.71075	80
	Control	21.1708	17.34178	120
	Total	25.1975	20.22467	200
Phase V	Experimental	38.3250	21.62571	80
	Control	24.2417	15.05368	120
	Total	29.8750	19.20968	200

The above data represent mean scores and standard deviations of students in both the experimental and control groups on CBM English reading aloud measures. The scores are the number words read correctly in 1 minute. Data from all five phases are included here.

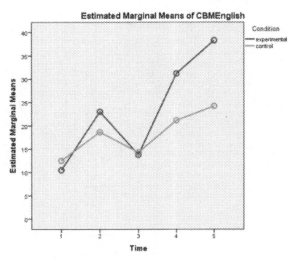

Figure 3. CBM English reading - Grade V

Below is the graphical representation of the mean scores across the five phases of data collection.

The blue line represents the number of words read correctly in the two model schools, while the green line represents the same metric for students in the four control schools.

5.5 Result 5-7: Split - plot repeated measures ANOVA for CBM English Reading

a. Split - plot repeated measures ANOVA for CBM English Reading - Grade III

Source	Time	Type III Sum of Squares	df	Mean Square	F	Sig.	Partial Eta Squared
Time	Linear	15328.79	1	15328.79	166.42	0.000	0.6
Time * Condition	Linear	4745.846	1	4745.846	51.524	0.000	0.317
Condition		4622.646	1	4622.646	17.41	0.000	0.136

b. Split - plot repeated measures ANOVA for CBM English Reading - Grade IV

Source	Time	Type III Sum of Squares	df	Mean Square	F	Sig.	Partial Eta Squared
Time	Linear	36456.99	1	36456.99	382.667	0.000	0.71
Time * Condition	Linear	9394.77	1	9394.77	98.611	0.000	0.387
Condition		13083.52	1	13083.52	18.219	0.000	0.105

c. **Split - plot repeated measures ANOVA for CBM English Reading - Grade V**

Source	Time	Type III Sum of Squares	df	Mean Square	F	Sig.	Partial Eta Squared
Time	Linear	38806.24	1	38806.24	603.658	0.000	0.753
Time * Condition	Linear	6921.324	1	6921.324	107.666	0.000	0.352
Condition		6466.74	1	6466.74	5.543	0.020	0.027

Results 5-7 in the above tables include statistics on the differences between slopes of oral reading fluency in English for all three grade levels. The results in the tables for students in grades 3-5 indicate that the students in the experimental group who participated in the Response to Intervention (RTI) approach significantly outperformed the students in the schools that did not implement RTI (control group).

5.6 Results 8-10: Math Computation

Math Computation ability of Grade III to V were assessed using Computation and comparison made between experimental and control groups using CBM probes prepared. The V phases of data collection indicate a class of students for example III Grade students participated Phase I to Phase III in the same Grade and IV & V phases of tests were administered when they moved to upper Grade (IV Grade). In the research it is considered as V phases of data for a single grade.

5.6.1 Result 8: Math Computation ability of Grade III

Data Collection Phase	Condition	Mean	Std. Deviation	N
Phase I	Experimental	5.1136	4.16500	44
	Control	5.0449	4.06057	78
	Total	5.0697	4.08146	122
Phase II	Experimental	8.5682	7.26939	44
	Control	6.8077	4.56642	78
	Total	7.4426	5.72446	122
Phase III	Experimental	10.2273	8.13509	44
	Control	9.4231	10.37513	78
	Total	9.7131	9.60047	122
Phase IV	Experimental	19.9318	11.45547	44
	Control	13.0769	9.41954	78
	Total	15.5492	10.67813	122
Phase V	Experimental	29.9205	10.44083	44
	Control	16.7244	10.19442	78
	Total	21.4836	12.05650	122

The above data represent mean scores and standard deviations of students in both the experimental and control groups on CBM math computation measures. The scores are the number of correct digits completed

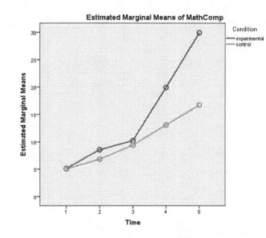

Figure 4. CBM Math Computation - Grade III

in 3 minutes. Data from all five phases are included here. Below are the graphical representations of the mean scores across the five phases of data collection.

The blue line represents the number of correct digits in the two model schools, while the green line represents the same metric for students in the four control schools.

Math Concept and Computation ability of Grade IV was assessed using between experimental and control groups.

5.6.2   Result 9: CBM Math Computation - Grade IV

Data Collection Phase	Condition	Mean	Std. Deviation	N
Phase I	Experimental	16.6418	11.90009	67
	Control	16.7151	12.04439	93
	Total	16.6844	11.94663	160
Phase II	Experimental	20.4030	11.15906	67
	Control	21.7903	13.58574	93
	Total	21.2094	12.60783	160
Phase III	Experimental	13.9030	7.54393	67
	Control	15.0538	9.76642	93
	Total	14.5719	8.89595	160
Phase IV	Experimental	19.5746	9.07889	67
	Control	19.3710	11.06549	93
	Total	19.4563	10.25054	160
Phase V	Experimental	27.1343	8.07051	67
	Control	21.5753	11.16963	93
	Total	23.9031	10.33412	160

The above data represent mean scores and standard deviations of students in both the experimental and control groups on CBM math computation measures. The scores are the number correct digits completed in 3 minutes. Data from all five phases are included here. Below is the graphical representations of the mean scores across the five phases of data collection.

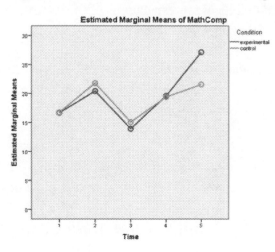

Figure 5. CBM Math Computation - Grade IV

The blue line represents the number of correct digits in the two model schools, while the green line represents the same metric for students in the four control schools.

Math Concept and Computation ability of Grade V was assessed using between experimental and control groups.

5.6.3 *Result 10: CBM Math Computation - Grade V*

Data Collection Phase	Condition	Mean	Std. Deviation	N
Phase I	Experimental	19.7069	11.71303	87
	Control	23.4880	10.13686	125
	Total	21.9363	10.94447	212
Phase II	Experimental	22.3046	11.04914	87
	Control	24.7960	9.22328	125
	Total	23.7736	10.06287	212
Phase III	Experimental	13.9368	6.42977	87
	Control	16.1920	6.58008	125
	Total	15.2665	6.59786	212
Phase IV	Experimental	20.9368	8.54972	87
	Control	20.6760	6.98162	125
	Total	20.7830	7.64559	212
Phase V	Experimental	26.1667	8.80528	87
	Control	21.6880	7.31069	125
	Total	23.5259	8.23934	212

The above data represent mean scores and standard deviations of students in both the experimental and control groups on CBM math computation measures. The scores are the number correct

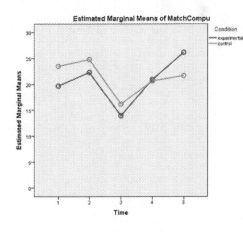

Figure 6. CBM Math Computation - Grade V

digits completed in 3 minutes. Data from all five phases are

103

included here. Below are the graphical representations of the mean scores across the five phases of data collection.

The blue line represents the number of correct digits in the two model schools, while the green line represents the same metric for students in the four control schools.

5.7 Results: 11-13: Split-plot repeated measures ANOVA for CBM

Result: 11: Math Computation - Grade III

Source	Time	Type III Sum of Squares	df	Mean Square	F	Sig.	Partial Eta Squared
Time	Linear	23093.85	1	23093.85	426.35	0.000	0.78
Time * Condition	Linear	2764.628	1	2764.628	51.04	0.000	0.298
Condition		2895.167	1	2895.167	13.461	0.000	0.101

Result 12: Split-plot repeated measures ANOVA for CBM Math Computation - Grade IV

Source	Time	Type III Sum of Squares	df	Mean Square	F	Sig.	Partial Eta Squared
Time	Linear	2936.087	1	2936.087	65.434	0.000	0.293
Time * Condition	Linear	643.614	1	643.614	14.344	0.000	0.083
Condition		77.35	1	77.35	0.169	0.681	0.001

Result 13: Split-plot repeated measures ANOVA for CBM Math Computation - Grade V

Source	Time	Type III Sum of Squares	df	Mean Square	F	Sig.	Partial Eta Squared
Time	Linear	75.315	1	75.315	1.769	0.185	0.008
Time * Condition	Linear	1905.174	1	1905.174	44.743	0.000	0.176
Condition		147.233	1	147.233	0.527	0.469	0.003

Results 11-13 include statistics on the differences between slopes of math computation for all three grade levels. The results in the table for students in grade 3 indicate that the students in the experimental group who participated in the Response to Intervention (RTI) approach significantly outperformed the students in the schools that did not implement RTI (control group). In grade 4, there was no statistical difference between the growth rate in math computation between the groups, even though they both improved significantly and there was a significant interaction between improvement and condition. In 5th grade, however, there was not significant improvement in math computation in either group as illustrated by Figure 6.

5.8 Results 14 -17 English Reading Ability – Phase II Intervention

5.8.1 Result 14: Testing Wise Mean, SD and t value for Oral Reading Fluency of Grade III Students (Phase II Intervention)

Progress Monitoring	Schools	ORF			
		N	M	SD	T
PM 1	2 Tier	17	5.82	4.066	5.42 (S)
	3 Tier	17	.41	.618	
PM 2	2 Tier	17	7.71	3.077	6.20 (S)
	3 Tier	16	2.50	1.549	
PM 3	2 Tier (17)	15	7.27	3.390	4.69 (S)
	3 Tier (17)	15	2.67	1.718	
PM 4	2 Tier (17)	16	12.13	5.987	6.40 (S)
	3 Tier (17)	16	2.31	1.352	
PM 5	2 Tier (17)	5	12.60	5.941	1.13 (NS)
	3 Tier (17)	7	9.43	2.299	

The above table states that the t values for the Oral Reading Fluency of Tier II & Tier III students studying in Grade III are significant in all five Progress Monitoring test. It indicates that tier 2 students secured higher score than Tier III students. However, the tier 3 students showed gradual improvement from Progress Monitoring 1 to Progress Monitoring 3.

5.8.2 Result 15: Testing Wise Mean, SD and t value for Oral Reading Fluency of Grade IV Students (Phase II Intervention)

Progress Monitoring	Schools	ORF			
		N	M	SD	t
PM 1	2 Tier (31)	31	7.35	5.444	6.05 (S)
	3 Tier (19)	18	.89	1.811	
PM 2	2 Tier (31)	31	13.68	9.537	6.59 (S)
	3 Tier (19)	18	2.00	1.940	
PM 3	2 Tier (31)	29	13.14	8.758	5.59 (S)
	3 Tier (19)	17	3.06	3.230	
PM 4	2 Tier (31)	26	15.96	12.466	4.98 (S)
	3 Tier (19)	15	3.20	2.957	
PM 5	2 Tier (31)	26	16.88	11.350	4.57 (S)
	3 Tier (19)	17	6.00	3.464	

From the above table it is evident ant that the t-values for Oral Reading Fluency is significant in all 5 progress monitoring tests. It indicate that Tier 2 students Grade IV has secured higher score than Tier 3 students of two experimental schools, However while comparing the scores of students from same Tier, indicate that both Tier 2 and Tier 3 students progressed from test1 to test5 Hence it is concluded that the intervention was found to be effective in enhancing the reading ability.

5.8.3 Result 16: Testing Wise Mean, SD and t value for Math Concept & Application and Computation of Grade III Students (Phase II Intervention)

Progress Moni-toring	Schools	Mathematics Concept & Applications				Mathematics Computations			
		N	M	SD	t	N	M	SD	t
PM 1	2 Tier (18)	18	1.44	1.464	2.55 (S)	18	12.39	7.039	4.74 (S)
	3 Tier (18)	18	0.44	.784		18	2.72	5.027	
PM 2	2 Tier (18)	14	3.64	2.437	3.03 (S)	14	16.21	6.278	6.76 (S)
	3 Tier (18)	18	1.33	1.680		18	3.44	3.682	
PM 3	2 Tier (18)	14	4.07	2.464	2.27 (S)	14	18.86	8.393	5.03 (S)
	3 Tier (18)	14	2.14	1.994		14	5.79	4.902	
PM 4	2 Tier (18)	13	5.31	3.425	3.22 (S)	13	28.31	11.331	5.38 (S)
	3 Tier (18)	16	2.00	1.549		16	7.44	9.352	
PM 5	2 Tier (18)	15	5.27	2.890	2.05 (S)	15	26.93	12.453	2.85 (S)
	3 Tier (18)	9	2.78	2.863		9	11.56	12.934	

From the above table it is evident that the t-values for Math Concept & Application and Math Computation is significant in all 5 progress monitoring tests. It indicate that Tier 2 students of Grade III has secured higher score than Tier 3 students of both Experimental School1 and Experimental School2, However while comparing the mean scores of students from same Tier, indicate that the students from both Tier 2 and Tier 3 progressed from test1 to test5 Hence it is concluded that the intervention was found to be effective in enhancing the math ability.

5.8.4 Result 17: Testing Wise Mean, SD and t value for Math Concept & Application and Computation of Grade IV Students (Phase II Intervention)

Progress Moni-toring	Schools	Mathematics Concept & Applications				Mathematics Computations			
		N	M	SD	t	N	M	SD	t
PM 1	2 Tier (21)	19	2.89	2.183	1.28 (NS)	19	16.53	6.141	4.30 (S)
	3 Tier (13)	13	1.85	2.304		13	6.00	7.200	
PM 2	2 Tier (21)	18	4.28	2.824	1.78 (NS)	18	25.83	9.395	3.22 (S)
	3 Tier (13)	13	2.69	2.136		13	14.00	10.591	
PM 3	2 Tier (21)	16	3.75	2.206	0.77 (NS)	16	22.63	10.105	2.64 (S)
	3 Tier (13)	13	2.92	3.353		13	12.46	10.485	
PM 4	2 Tier (21)	15	4.93	2.374	3.14 (S)	15	25.00	11.116	2.66 (S)
	3 Tier (13)	11	2.36	1.804		12	14.58	9.268	
PM 5	2 Tier (21)	14	4.50	2.410	1.15 (NS)	14	24.36	10.938	1.58 (NS)
	3 Tier (13)	10	3.30	2.584		10	18.00	8.667	

From the above table it is evident that the t-values for Math Concept and Application is significant in Test 4 and for Math Concept & Application is significant I Test 1 to 4. It indicates that Tier 2 Grade IV students has secured higher score than Tier 3 students in Test 2 for Math Concept & Application and Test1 to Test4 for Math Computation. However while comparing the mean scores of students from same Tier, indicate that both Tier 2 and Tier 3 students had steady progress from Test 1 to Test 5 for both Math Concept & Application and Math Computation. Hence it is concluded that the intervention was found to be effective in enhancing the math ability.

5.9 Result 18: Progress Monitoring: Grade IV Tier 3 students of Experimental School

Student ID	Oral Reading Fluency Score		
	PM 1	PM 2	PM 3
01	1	2	1
02	4	5	7
03	3	6	10
04	5	7	9
05	0	0	
06	2	6	9
07	8	10	13
08	6	9	13
Mean	**5.3**	**7.2**	**10.2**

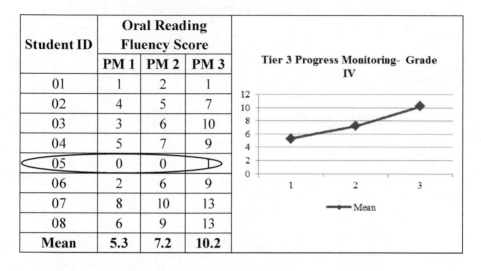

The students who did not show the progress even after 3 months intervention, they were referred to Special Education services. Other than the student with ID 5 the mean scores have been calculated & it was steadily increasing and the progress is represented graphically.

5.10 Result 19: Progress Monitoring: Grade III Tier 3 students of Experimental School 2

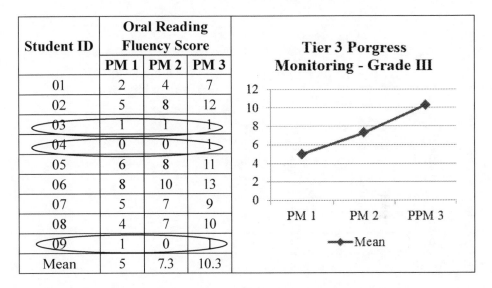

Student ID	Oral Reading Fluency Score		
	PM 1	PM 2	PM 3
01	2	4	7
02	5	8	12
03	1	1	1
04	0	0	1
05	6	8	11
06	8	10	13
07	5	7	9
08	4	7	10
09	1	0	
Mean	5	7.3	10.3

The students who did not show the progress even after 3 months intervention they were referred to Special Education services. Other than these students with ID 3, 4 and 9 the mean score have been calculated & it was steadily increasing and the progress is represented graphically.

5.11 Result 20: Progress Monitoring: Grade III Tier 3 students of Experimental School 1

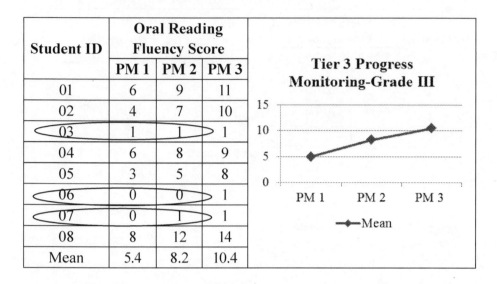

Student ID	Oral Reading Fluency Score		
	PM 1	PM 2	PM 3
01	6	9	11
02	4	7	10
03	1	1	1
04	6	8	9
05	3	5	8
06	0	0	1
07	0	1	1
08	8	12	14
Mean	5.4	8.2	10.4

The students who did not show the progress even after 3 months intervention they were referred to Special Education services. Other than these students with ID 3, 6 and 8 the mean scores have been calculated & it was steadily increasing and the progress is represented graphically.

5.12 RTI has impact on School Attendance of Students

In the RTI Schools, attendance was noted for two Phases of Intervention. The following table shows the results.

5.12.1 Result 21: Percentage Analysis on Absenteeism of Experimental School 1

Grade	Total No. of Students	Absentees															
		Phase I (June - Nov 2015)								Phase II (Jan - Mar 2016)							
		0-5		6-10		11-15		16-20		0-5		6-10		11-15		16-20	
		No	%	No	%	No	%	No	%	No	%	No	%	No	%	No	%
I	32	4	12.5	15	47	9	28	4	12.5	16	50	14	44	2	6	0	0
II	37	7	19	8	22	16	43	6	16	12	32	17	46	7	19	1	3
III	38	11	29	11	29	11	29	5	13	19	50	15	39	3	8	1	3
IV	36	6	17	12	33	14	39	4	11	18	49	15	42	2	6	1	3
V	48	20	42	18	37	9	19	1	2	30	62	15	32	2	4	1	2

The impact of RTI on reduction of absentees was analyzed considering II and III Phases of the Project. In the First Phase, for example in Grade 3, 16-20 days absentees were 13 % whereas it was 3 % at the end of

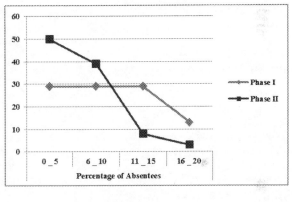

2nd Phase. In the II Phase, between 0-5 days absentees, were 50 % and in the Phase I was 29% indicating influence of RTI on attendance of the students and that is represented graphically.

5.12.2 Result 22: Percentage Analysis on Absenteeism of Experimental School 2

Grade	Total No. of Students	Absentees															
		Phase I (June - Nov 2015)								Phase II (Jan - Mar 2016)							
		0-5		6-10		11-15		16-20		0-5		6-10		11-15		16-20	
		No	%	No	%	No	%	No	%	No	%	No	%	No	%	No	%
I	22	3	14	6	27	7	32	6	27	8	36	7	32	5	23	2	9
II	27	5	18	8	30	7	26	7	26	8	30	9	33	6	22	4	15
III	32	10	31	13	41	5	16	4	12	18	56	9	28	4	13	1	3
IV	54	4	7	17	32	21	39	12	22	14	26	27	50	10	19	3	5
V	52	17	33	22	42	8	15	5	10	34	65	13	25	4	8	1	2

The impact of RTI on reduction of absentees was analyzed considering I and II Phases of the Project. In the First Phase, for example in Grade 4, 16-20 days absentees were 22 % whereas it was 5 % at the end of 2nd Phase. In the II Phase, between 0-5 days, were 50 % in the I Phase and it was 25 %

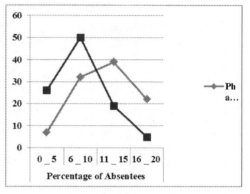

in 1st Phase indication influence of RTI on attendance of the students and that is represented graphically.

5.13 Discussion

Overall, the project results are very positive and encouraging, especially for English and Tamil reading. Students in the two model schools who entered the RTI project the earliest (in 1st grade) as opposed to in later grades, demonstrated the most significant improvements in all academic areas. When considering students receiving Tier 1, 2 or 3 interventions, it was demonstrated that students in Tier 3 generally showed the steepest learning curve, even though they did not grow by as many correct words or digits. Students in Tiers 2 and 1 grew at approximately the same rate even though the initial assessments showed Tier 2 students performing at lower levels.

The core curriculum (SABL) that is being taught in Tamil Nadu corporation and government-aided schools is not meeting the needs of a large percentage of learners, especially in English reading and math. This can be either due to the fact that the curriculum is not being implement as intended or that the content of curriculum is not sufficient to produce successful learning. Another potential reason for the lack of success of the curriculum implementation is: a) it does not teach reading as a specific skill, but rather as part of general language development, and b) many of the teachers do speak English at a level as to help students become fluent English readers.

RTI is a systems-level intervention that takes time (at least 1 -2 years) to implement well to see significant results. RTI implementation includes several stages, starting from planning, training teachers in Tier 2 and 3 interventions and understand of assessment data, preparation of assessment and teaching materials, to frequent monitoring of student progress to modify instruction.

There were only 16 students in the study with identified disabilities, i.e. hearing impairments, intellectual disabilities and ADHD. Many students with disabilities in South India, especially those with more severe disabilities, do not attend regular schools, even though India has adopted the Education for All (EFA) philosophy and legislation. Many students with disabilities do not have a way to get to school and the schools are not prepared well to teach them. On the other hand, there are struggling students in the corporation and government-aided schools who do not have a disability label. This fact is in certain ways an advantage over the disability identification approaches in Western countries. Students who learn at different paces in South India are expected to be educated alongside their peers. For these students, the RTI approach is especially useful and practical as they can be assisted and their learning accelerated without having to a disability label. It was observed during the project, that there is a shortage of special educators and other teaching specialists in the type of schools we worked in.

The project results have several implications: 1. Response to Intervention (RTI) has been demonstrated to be a promising school-wide intervention in helping students from low socio-economic backgrounds who are not performing academically as their peers to improve in reading and math; 2. The SABL curriculum and its implementation should be examined to make sure that it is a viable pedagogical tool to educating all students effectively; 3. It is important to start intervening with children who are lagging behind to improve their basic academic skills as soon as possible after they enter school; 4. Formative assessment, i.e. CBM, is a critical tool in determining whether a child is performing on par with his or her peers and to monitor their progress; 5. There is a need for general and special education teachers/other teaching specialists to work together to better address the needs of diverse learners.

Impacts

The project analyzed marked effect or influence based on the outcomes for sustainability. This evidence based research has impact in various dimensions.

Scientific Impact

This project is of theoretical and empirical significance to scientific community. The theoretical impact of the study lies in describing the curriculum Based measurement which is a new entity in the Indian context. The study demonstrates validated reading and math assessment tools which have all the psychometric properties and can be widely used/ adopted in Indian context.

Empirically this study is important in helping researchers and scientific community to better understand the method of administering tools and techniques of engaging students minute to minute and keep all students in the class on the job (learning). This research set a benchmarking of tests procedure for whole school screening and every child has a place in the school. The research stands evidence that when RTI is implemented effectively, students with academic difficulties can be identified and intervened before the academic gap widens and thus developing a new paradigm which will be adopted in other parts of the countries. Researchers already started doing further researches in this area. RTI courses are introduced as a professional certificate course at Avninashilingam Institute for Home science and Higher Education for Women in collaboration with ICI, University of Minnesota, Minneapolis, USA. Efforts are being made to introduce the course online.

Capacity Impact

Quality improvement is evidenced among stakeholders.

a. The capacity of the teachers to teach core instruction in the classroom was built and the teachers are able to handle the class with tiered instruction when necessary.
b. Capacity of the teacher trainees was built and in turn they introduce multi- tier approach in the respective school they work
c. Capacity of teacher educators was enhanced at national level and there is a scope for more researches and implementation of tiered system across the country
d. Nearly 410 students enhance their reading and math skills in this three year project and it has a long term impact in their education.
e. The capacity of the project team was built and the team can act as researchers and practitioners and the knowledge and expertise can be disseminated widely

Social Impact

a. This project emphasizes that students should be addressed to meet their learning needs against simply branding children at the initial stage itself that he/ she is with sensory or cognitive disability. Every child is a child fist. The teaching should address the diverse needs of the children. After 3months of intervention and 6 progress monitoring if a student is not showing improvement, then the student will be referred for special education services. This concept is against the prevalent concept pointing the child first its disability then addressing his/her needs.

b. Reading math ability is enhanced among students. The students in Experimental schools showed better academic performance than students in Control schools.

c. Absentees rate were reduced from 13% to 2% at the end of the Project and thus dropout rate is less than 2%.

d. Development of RTI model was field tested and has become a new paradigm in Indian context to be adopted for all children learning.

e. Indo- Us research collaboration is being sustained on both sides in terms of collaborative activities such scholar exchange (efforts made), further research collaboration.

Reference

1. Batsche, G., Elliott, J., Graden, J. L., Grimes, J., Kovaleski, J. F., Prasse, D., et al. (2005). *Response to Intervention Policy Considerations and Implementation*. Reston, VA: National Association of State Directors of Special Education.

Glossary

B
Benchmark
It is the process of screening all students on essential skills predictive of later academic performance and should be completed three or four times per year (quarterly). The testing should be administered in a standardized format, which often works best when the same group of individuals completes the testing for all three benchmarks. Benchmark testing should always be done at grade-level.

Blending phoneme words
It involves pulling together individual sounds or syllables within *words*; Have students put together *phonemes* to create *words* and break down.

C
Core instruction
It provided to all students in the general education classroom. Those instructional strategies that are used routinely with all students in a general-education setting.

Curriculum
It is defined as the lessons and academic content taught in a school or in a specific course or program.

Curriculum-Based Measurement
It is a set of standardized and validated short duration tests that are used by special education and general education teachers for the purpose of evaluating the effects of their instructional programs in the basic skills of reading, mathematics computation, spelling, and written expression.

Consequential validity
It describes the after effects and possible social and societal results from a particular assessment or measure. For an assessment to have consequential validity it must not have negative social consequences

that seem abnormal. If this occurs it signifies the test isn't valid and is not measuring things accurately. Consequential validity can help identify tests that are not measuring things they are supposed to be measuring or that it is falsely measuring those actually taking it.

D

Data analysis

It is a process of inspecting, cleansing, transforming, and modeling data with the goal of discovering useful information, suggesting conclusions, and supporting decision-making.

Data based decision making

It refers to educator's ongoing process of collecting and analyzing different types of data, including demographic, student achievement test, satisfaction, process data to guide decisions towards improvement of educational process. DDDM helps to recognize the problem and who is affected by the problem; therefore, DDDM can find a solution of the problem.

Differentiated Instruction

It means tailoring instruction to meet individual needs. Whether teachers differentiate content, process, products, or the learning environment, the use of ongoing assessment and flexible grouping makes this a successful approach to instruction.

F

Flesh Reading

Ease formula is a simple approach to assess the grade level of the reader.

G

General education

Basic coursework program for post-secondary schools and it refers to the educational foundation of skills, knowledge, habits of mind, and values that prepares students for success in their majors and in their personal and professional lives.

General Education Teacher

He/She having sole responsibility for all the students in the class.

Guided Reading

It can be defined as a practice in which you, as the teacher, assist your students in navigating the reading process.

H

High Quality Instruction

Children receive instruction that follows a scope and sequence. Instruction is differentiated within the classroom to meet a broad range of student needs.

High Frequency Words

These are the most commonly occurring words in print. Reading probes are scored according to words correctly read aloud per minute. Reading probes are scored according to the number of words correctly read.

I

Intervention

It is based on student needs. Interventions supplement the general education curriculum. Interventions are a systematic compilation of well researched or evidence-based specific instructional strategies and techniques.

Instruction

It is vital for education, as it is the transfer of learning from one person to another and activities that impart knowledge or skill.

Instructional Intervention

An instructional intervention is a specific program or set of steps to help a child improve in an area of need.

Intensive Interventions

At this level, students receive individualized, intensive interventions that target the students' skill deficits.

Instructional Modification

An Instructional Modification is a change to the content to make it more accessible to students who are struggling.

L

Letter Naming Fluency (LNF)

It is a standardized, individually administered test that provides a measure of risk and assesses the ability to recognize and name a random mixture of uppercase and lowercase letters.

Lesson Plan

A lesson plan is a detailed guide for teaching a lesson. Creating a lesson plan involves setting goals, developing activities, and determining the materials that will be used. Lessons are organized by subject and grade level. Within each lesson, you will find clear objectives, description of materials needed, a thorough procedure with an opening and a closing, as well as assessments and modifications.

M

Math Conept

A **math concept** is the 'why' or 'big idea' of math.

Math Computation

In math, a computation method is used to find an answer in regards to any given problem. The most common computation methods make up the majority of basic math functions including addition, subtraction, multiplication and division.

Math probe

It consists of single- and multiple-skill worksheets and have a two-minute time limit.

Maze Passage

Curriculum-based measurement (CBM) Maze passages are timed measures that measure reading comprehension. They are better predictors of future reading performance than CBM oral reading fluency probes. Students read Maze passages silently during assessment, so Maze can be administered to a whole class at one time. Passages used for Maze should be at least 300 words in length.

Modifications

It is provided to students with an Individualized Education Program (IEP), and focus on the alteration of the structure of curricular materials. A modification changes the expectations of what a student is expected to know or do -typically by lowering the academic standards against which the student is to be evaluated.

O

Oral Reading Fluency (ORF)

It measures a student's reading fluency by having that student read aloud for 1 minute from a prepared passage. During the student's reading, the examiner makes note of any reading errors in the passage. Then the examiner scores the passage by calculating the number of words read correctly.

P

Probe

It contains a mixture of problems that represent skills to be mastered by the end of the year. In each academic area, probes are developed (e.g. brief reading passages, short spelling lists, samples of math items from the curriculum, etc.) and these probes are used to collect data on student performance. These probes are developed from the books or materials that make up the child's curriculum.

Progress Monitoring

A scientifically based practice that is used to frequently assess students' performance and evaluate the effectiveness of instruction. Data that indicates a substantial lack of progress signals the need for more intensive interventions that match the skill deficit.

Psychometric Properties

It is the construction and validation of measurement instruments and assessing if these instruments are reliable and valid forms of measurement. **Practicality**: Something that demonstrates *practicality* makes good sense. The practicalities of a situation are the practical aspects of it, as opposed to its theoretical aspects.

Phoneme

A set of phonetically similar but slightly differing sounds in a language that are heard as the same sound by native speakers and are represented in phonemic transcription by the same symbol: in

English, the *phoneme*/p/ includes the phonetically differentiated sounds represented by *p* in "pin," "spin," and "tip"

Partner Reading

It is a cooperative learning strategy in which two students work together to read an assigned text. The Partner Reading strategy allows students to take turns reading and provide each other with feedback as a way to monitor comprehension.

R

Readability Statistics

Readability statistics measure text features that are subject to mathematical calculations such as number of syllables and sentence length for reading ease and reading Grade level.

Regular Classroom

A room or place especially in a school in which classes are conducted

Response to Intervention (RTI)

It is a multi-tier approach to the early identification and support of students with learning and behavior needs. The RTI process begins with high-quality instruction and universal screening of all children in the general education classroom. Struggling learners are provided with interventions at increasing levels of intensity to accelerate their rate of learning.

Reading Comprehension

Comprehending the passage at the first reading

S

Sarva Shiksha Abhiyan (SSA)

It is a Hindi language term meaning Education For All. It is a programme for Universal Elementary Education. This programme is also an attempt to provide an opportunity for improving human capabilities to all children through provision of community -owned quality education in a mission mode. It is a response to the demand for quality basic education all over the country.

Simplified Activity Based Learning (SABL)

It is aimed at cultivating self-learning skills and allows children to bring out his aptitude and skill that is hidden in them. Children learn from each other practically that leads to participate, understand and exchange ideas. The children are facilitated by the teachers through innovative activities.

Special education

It is a form of instruction that's designed to meet the needs of students with disabilities, so that they can learn the same skills and information as other children in school. The term special education is used interchangeably with special needs, and the disabilities may be physical, emotional, or behavioral.

Special Educator

Teacher is someone who works with children and youths who have a variety of disabilities. Children with special needs require unique instruction by specially trained professionals to help them achieve their highest potential and strive to progress beyond their limitations.

Supplementary Instruction

It either reinforces what has been already been taught, or it attaches new instruction to what has been taught while it may be prescribed by an instructor or program, or voluntarily selected by a learner, the intent is to either reteach or enhance existing instruction.

T

The Flesch Reading Ease Formula

It is a simple approach to assess the grade-level of the reader. It's also one of the few accurate measures around that we can rely on without too much scrutiny. This formula is best used on school text.

Tier 1 Instruction

All students in Tier 1 receive high-quality, scientifically based instruction, differentiated to meet their needs, and are screened on a periodic basis to identify struggling learners who need additional support.

Tier 2: Targeted Interventions

In Tier 2, students not making adequate progress in the core curriculum are provided with increasingly intensive instruction matched to their needs on the basis of levels of performance and rates of progress.

Tier 3: Intensive Interventions and Comprehensive Evaluation

At this level, students receive individualized, intensive interventions that target the students' skill deficits for the remediation of existing problems and the prevention of more severe problems.

Tiered Instruction

A multi-tier approach is used to efficiently differentiate instruction for all students. The model incorporates increasing intensities of instruction offering specific, research-based interventions matched to student needs.

U

Universal Screening

Universal screening is the first step in identifying the students who are at risk for learning difficulties. It is a central component of all RTI models is early screening of all students to identify those at risk for academic and/or behavior difficulties.

Printed in the United States
By Bookmasters